The Ulm Campaign 1805

The Ulm Campaign 1805

Napoleon and the Defeat of the Austrian Army During the 'War of the Third Coalition'

F. N. Maude

The Ulm Campaign 1805: Napoleon and the Defeat of the Austrian Army During the 'War of the Third Coalition'
by F. N. Maude

Published by Leonaur Ltd

ISBN: 978-1-84677-404-1 (hardcover)
ISBN: 978-1-84677-403-4 (softcover)

http://www.leonaur.com

Publisher's Notes

Contents

Maps

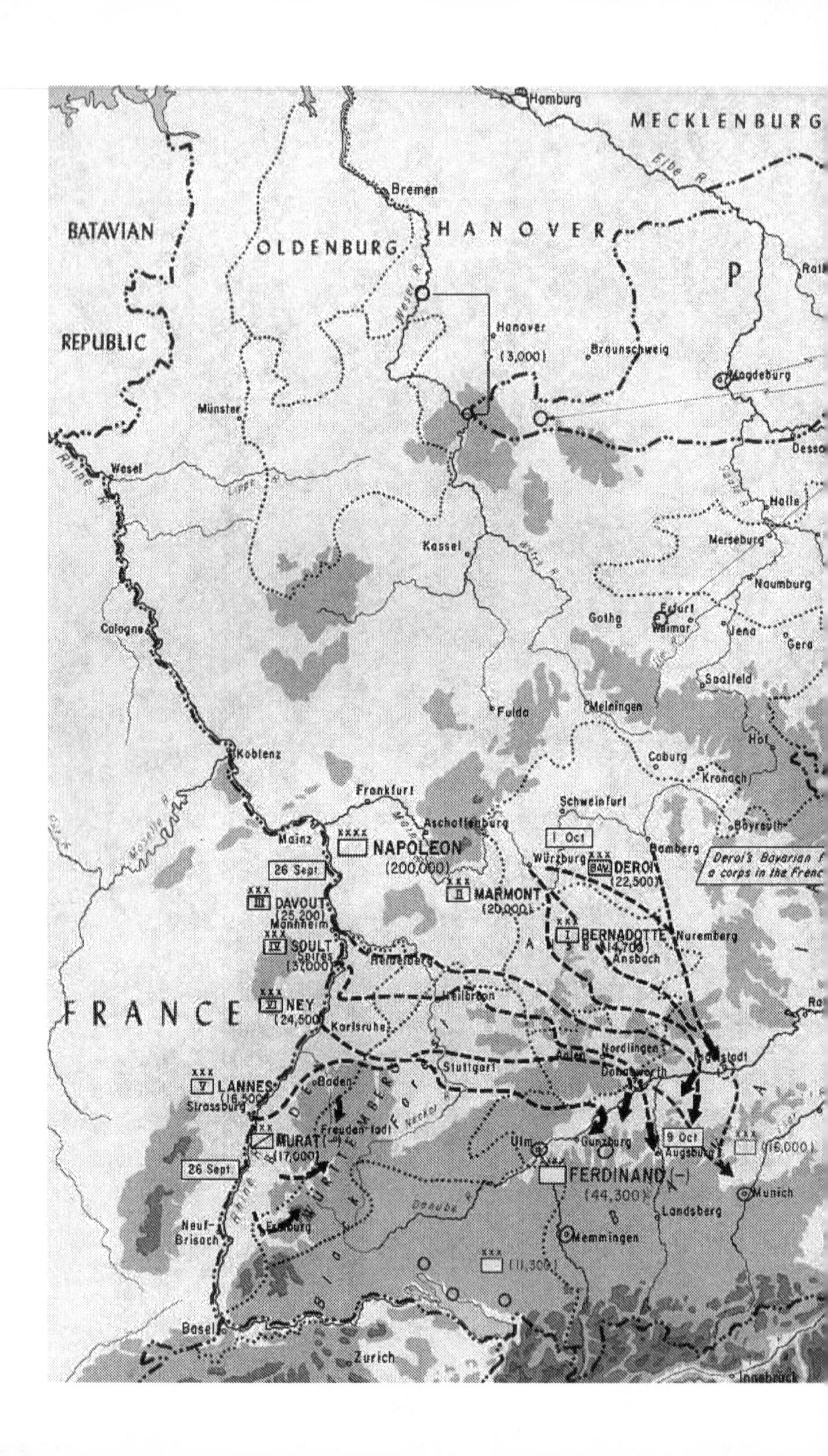

Hamburg
MECKLENBURG
Elbe R.
Bremen
BATAVIAN
REPUBLIC
OLDENBURG
HANOVER
P
Hanover
(3,000)
Braunschweig
Magdeburg
Münster
Wesel
Rhine R.
Lippe R.
Halle
Merseburg
Kassel
Naumburg
Gotha
Erfurt
Weimar
Jena
Gera
Cologne
Saalfeld
Fulda
Meiningen
Hof
Koblenz
Coburg
Kronach
Frankfurt
Schweinfurt
Aschaffenburg
Bayreuth
Mainz
NAPOLEON
(200,000)
1 Oct
Würzburg
Bamberg
Deroi's Bavarian
a corps in the Franc
26 Sept.
DEROI
(22,500)
DAVOUT
(25,200)
Mannheim
MARMONT
(20,000)
SOULT
Spires
(37,000)
BERNADOTTE
Nuremberg
Ansbach
Heilbronn
FRANCE
NEY
(24,500)
Karlsruhe
Nordlingen
Ingolstadt
Stuttgart
Donauwörth
LANNES
(16,500)
Strassburg
Baden
Neckar
MURAT
(17,000)
Freudenstadt
9 Oct
Ulm
Gunzburg
Augsburg
(16,000)
26 Sept.
FERDINAND (-)
(44,300)
Munich
Danube
Landsberg
Neuf-Brisach
Freiburg
Memmingen
(11,300)
Basel
Zurich
Innsbruck

Stettin
Oder R.
Thorn
Vistula R.
Warsaw
50 miles
Berlin
U S S I A
Kustrin
Posen
Warthe R.
Frankfurt
Spree R.
IAN FORCES MOBILIZING
Lodz
Kalisch
Oder R.
Torgau
Liegnitz
Breslau
Görlitz
Dresden
Schweidnitz
BUXHÖWDEN
(38,000)
Reichenberg
Glatz
7 Oct.
Krakow
28 miles
22 Sept
Karlsbad
Prague
Kolin
Pilsen
Olmutz
A U S T R I A
Brunn
Austerlitz
Budweis
Znaim
March R.
Hollabrun
Passau
Krems
(20,000)
Vienna
Pressburg
KUTUSOV
Danube R.
Linz
St. Pölten
Amstetten
9 Oct.
Salzburg
Leoben
Graz
THE ULM CAMPAIGN
26th September -- 9th October 1805
ELEVATIONS IN METERS
SCALE OF MILES
N

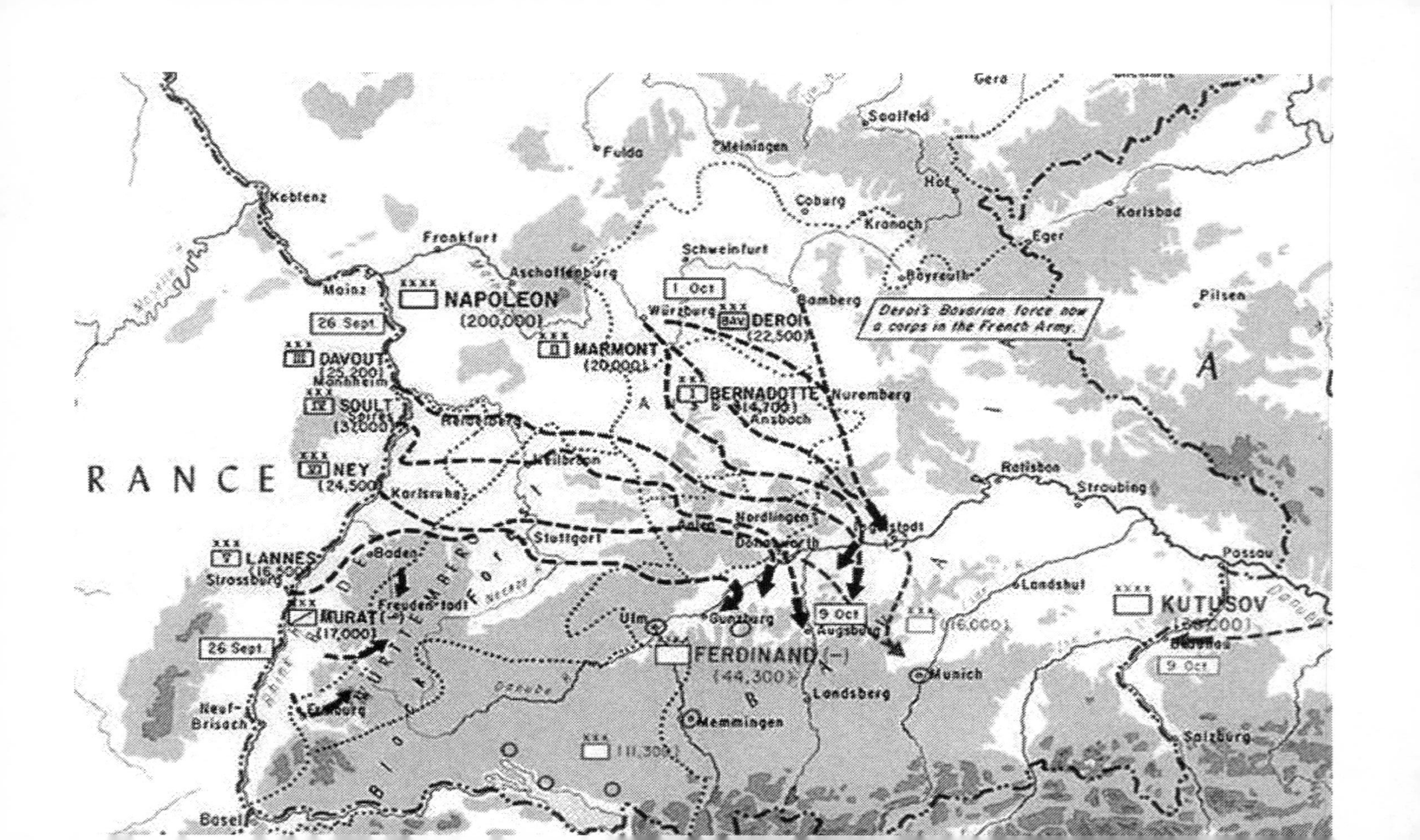
RANCE
NAPOLEON
(200,000)
26 Sept.
DAVOUT
(25,200)
SOULT
NEY
(24,500)
LANNES
MURAT (–)
(17,000)
26 Sept.
MARMONT
(20,000)
1 Oct
DEROI
(22,500)
BERNADOTTE
Deroi's Bavarian force now a corps in the French Army.
FERDINAND (–)
(44,300)
9 Oct
(16,000)
KUTUSOV
9 Oct
(11,300)
Koblenz
Mainz
Mannheim
Frankfurt
Aschaffenburg
Fulda
Meiningen
Saalfeld
Gera
Hof
Coburg
Kronach
Schweinfurt
Würzburg
Bamberg
Bayreuth
Eger
Karlsbad
Pilsen
Nuremberg
Ansbach
Heilbronn
Karlsruhe
Stuttgart
Nordlingen
Aalen
Donauwörth
Ratisbon
Straubing
Passau
Landshut
Strassburg
Baden
Freudenstadt
Ulm
Gunzburg
Augsburg
Munich
Landsberg
Memmingen
Salzburg
Neuf-Brisach
Basel
Danube
Neckar
Rhine
A
B

Introduction

A few words of explanation are necessary to justify my production of the three studies: Leipzig, Jena, Ulm, in the inverse order of their dates.

At the time I commenced the series, it appeared to me to be of the first importance to make it clear to my fellow-students that Napoleon did in fact possess during his latter years a fixed method in strategy, which he invariably followed whenever topographical conditions permitted. This method enabled him to be absolutely certain of accumulating at the decisive point of the battlefield a crushing numerical superiority, no matter what plans his opponents might have formed; for the vigour of his operations paralysed their will power and compelled them to conform to his initiative.

His calculations might indeed be destroyed by tactical incidents on the battlefield, as they were, both at Leipzig and Waterloo; but the strategic object viz. the concentration of superior numbers at the point of decision was invariably obtained, and by the simplest possible means.

The next step seemed to me to show how the new system first came into being during the Campaign of Jena, in which the uncertainty of the Emperor's leading gave the best possible proof of the novelty of the weapon he was learning how to wield in contrast to the certainty with which he handled it thereafter.

I should probably have rested at this point for good but

for the growing tendency I have noticed in recent strategical articles at home and abroad, to read this Napoleonic system into everything he ever did, rather suggesting that the idea was born with him, than that it was, as I believe, the outcome of his experience, developed logically and step by step.

To my mind the Campaign of Ulm, which was in fact his first essay in the conduct of a great army, articulated in Corps and Divisions, proves my point up to the hilt.

In Italy he followed the methods of his predecessors, only departing from them in so far as the conditions of the troops he commanded, and their habits of living by requisition eked out by plunder, rendered expedient. But in South Germany all was different.

There for the first time we find a number of Corps, each an Army in magnitude according to the standard of the previous century, moving under the inspiration of a single leader and needing on the one hand space for subsistence, on the other, time to ensure concentration. A Cavalry Screen far out to the front was the first and obvious solution, and one to which the rest of Europe has absolutely adhered until the begining of the 20th century. It is the primary object of this present study to reveal its shortcomings.

I had originally intended merely to translate the introduction to the French Official History by M. Colin and d'Alombert, but our points of view differed so diametrically, especially with regard to the ability of Mack and the conduct of the Archduke Ferdinand, that I abandoned the idea, and determined to unravel as far as possible the fundamental causes which lay at the root of the whole series of defeats the Austrians endured at the hands of the French, from the very inception of the French Revolution.

I have never been able to share the views of those who imagine that every defeated General is necessarily either an imbecile or a traitor. In times of chronic warfare men do not easily win the confidence of their Sovereigns and contemporaries, and without this confidence it is utterly impossible for them to rise to high positions.

Mack and his contemporaries, both in the British, the Prussian, and his own army, were no mere carpet knights, but men who had grown up amongst the generation that had fought its way through the Seven Years' War, and during their own lifetime had spent as many years in face of the enemy as their successors now spend weeks at their autumn manoeuvres.

If, in spite of this practical training, they were again and again overwhelmed by defeat, the presumption is strong that they were in reality face to face with fresh and, to them, unknown causes, whose introduction into the problems they encountered entirely vitiated all previous practice. The time in which this practice was first evolved had been in fact the highest development of the Art of War as defined by von Moltke *viz.* "to make the best practicable use of the means at hand to the attainment of the object in view."

No one has ever, to my knowledge, turned the problem around and endeavoured to apply the Napoleonic methods to the conditions of Frederick the Great's day had they done so, the explanation would have stared them in the face.

Frederick's men needed no " lozenge " formations, not merely because his armies were small in number, but because it was an economic necessity of his period to win by individual efficiency and not by sheer weight of numbers.

Men so highly drilled that they could stand up to fifty per cent of loss, still loading and firing at the rate of five rounds a minute, needed no heavy reserves to support them in an attack. Their fire swept the ground in front of them like the very scythe of death, and, after three or four volleys, there was no enemy left to meet the shock of the bayonet charge. The same was the case with their Cavalry; charging knee to knee, without even squadron intervals, the longest front was bound to overwhelm all opponents, hence again there was no need to keep material reserves in hand.

But when, at the outbreak of the French Revolution, men with far less drill and steadiness than our present day troops, had to be led against a well-trained enemy, new methods had to be found to overcome that enemy's resistance, and only when these were fixed by experiment, did the motive for concentration of numbers on the decisive point spring into prominence.

Chapter 1
The Austrian Army

The evolution of the Austrian Army deserves far closer attention than it has hitherto received in this country, because in no other one belonging to the Western nations can the process of growth under uniform conditions be more thoroughly studied. The British Army has rarely fought twice within the same theatre of war during a generation of a soldier's life say twenty-five years; the French fighting organisation has twice been rent from end to end and reconstructed once in the absolute presence of overwhelming enemies and once at least the Prussians have had to undergo the same experience. But in Austria, even after the misfortunes of 1805 and 1809, no-violent break with the past ever took place, until after Sadowa. Even then, though the methods of filling the ranks and the term of service within them were profoundly modified, the regiments essentially remained, and one can trace their gradual evolution by successive small adaptations to the changes in their environment, from the days of Wallenstein and Tilly, and even earlier amongst the freebooters and *condottieri* of Sir John Hawkwood's time.

Essentially the defence of her frontiers rested, as in all feudal countries, upon the duty of every able-bodied man to serve, under his immediate overlord, in emergencies. But in the days when War was a chronic condition of existence, and the trade of handling weapons one which required almost a lifetime to master, the system, except on the frontiers adjacent to her less civilised neighbour, had fallen, as in other countries, almost completely into abeyance, and the levies it provided had been replaced by a professional force of regulars, which, having begun by being purely "mercenary," as the skilled labour employed by contractors today is also mercenary, had gradually, as the tradition of the regiments evolved itself, grown into a voluntary Army,[1] much as our own Army still remains in spite of our shorter service.

Originally the several commands had been raised by the "contract" system. The Monarch applied to some well-known soldier of fortune to raise a certain number of men, and to command them in the field for a specified purpose and rate of remuneration; then by a process of survival certain leaders and their followers acquired an established reputation. The chiefs were rewarded by grants of land, then settling the pick of their men around them, the commands gradually struck root into the country and became identified with specific territorial districts. The sons of these men grew up in the traditions of the regiments and in due time came forward as willing recruits, whilst there was always a fairly constant interchange between the men on the frontiers, who hankered after the regular serv-

1. On the close of the Seven Years' War much attention was devoted to improving the system of keeping up the numerical strength of the Army. By an order dated 9th May 1763, conscription with substitutes was introduced, the term of service being indefinite, practically for life. This proved unsatisfactory, and in 1770 the Prussian "Canton" system was introduced. In this the country was divided into regimental districts or "cantons," each bound to find a given number of troops with recourse to the ballot if necessary, and each district kept a reserve of 640 men on indefinite furlough at call. The Cavalry appear to have relied on voluntary enlistment. In 1792 Mack spoke of the Austrian system in the following terms: "No recruit is taken whose service is wanted for productive labours; on the other hand, no able-bodied man escapes who can be spared from them," an ideal perhaps rarely attained. Max Jahns states "the annual wastage was small, only 20 per cent." According to this the death-rate must have been about three times as high as in the pre-Mutiny days in India, when it stood at 6 per cent. See *Geschichte der Kriegswissenschaften*, vol. iii.

ice, and the bolder spirits of the plains who longed to get out into the world. The frontiersmen of Austria were, in fact, to the Austrian Army, very much what the Pathans and Afridis are to the Indian Army of the Victorian era. The presence of these wilder spirits necessitated a stern discipline. This welded the units into admirable machines for the old linear form of fighting, but it destroyed the individuality of the men.

Continuity of tradition, the semi-feudal type of command, and territorial connection, all these tended to make the Army exceedingly conservative and susceptible of restraint; but it was precisely this docility which handicapped it most when it came into collision with the new methods of the French Revolution.

It is necessary here to go back a long way to establish what the old methods of Continental armies really were, and how they had arisen, for the British Army by whose traditions English writers are naturally disposed to judge all military events from the nature of its service, never fought long enough in any one district to become thoroughly saturated with its local conditions. India and America were always there to correct any wide departure from the primitive principles of War, and our failure to realise Continental standpoints has sterilised nine-tenths of the efforts of our critics and historians, more particularly as regards the period now before us. Now without this basis of knowledge it is quite impossible to estimate fairly the difficulties with which all ranks of the Austrian Army had to contend, and the very real skill which some of their leaders showed in their endeavours to master them.

The keynote of the whole situation lay in the hold which the so-called "Laws of Warfare" had obtained over the minds of all classes during the eighteenth century, and these laws originated in the following manner. Before the horrors of the Thirty Years' War had reached their culminating point, a strong reaction against pushing the principles of War to their utmost logical conclusion had already set in amongst all the higher intellects of Europe, and many protests had been published. The chief of these sprang from the pen of Grotius, a learned Dutch jurist, and was entitled *De Bello ac Pace*. Its object was to mitigate the suffering of War, both for combatants and non-combatants, by mutual agreement between belligerents, and ever since then it has formed the foundation of existing codes of International Law. It met with considerable support, but the devils of cruelty and rapacity in the combatants had been thoroughly roused, and being now no longer restrained by the old custom of holding prisoners to ransom, it needed the accumulation of suffering which the next fifteen years so abundantly provided before "expediency," not "humanity," stepped in and compelled moderation.

By this time the whole of Central Europe had become such a desert that normal operations of War were practically impossible. Only fast-moving bodies could find subsistence along their lines of march, while the need of rapid mobility practically compelled the abandonment of the heavy artillery and siege material which alone could ensure the reduction of fortresses. Hence every hamlet and chateau developed walls and ramparts, and at the first sign of an approaching command the peasants—everywhere against the combatants—drove off what cattle they had to the forests, and for themselves took refuge within the walled towns which soon grew up under the shelter of the older castles.

Organised operations thus became an impossibility, and the War died of sheer inanition. Then began the process of reconstruction, and the first thing needed was the erection of an armed police, capable of dealing with the hordes of deserters and disbanded marauders who preyed on everyone alike. This police force was constituted from the most loyal and disciplined men of the old armies, and as long as the necessity of their services was felt the civil population not only co-operated with them gratefully, but were even thankful for the protection which they afforded. But peace settled down again, and as usual—*God was neglected and the soldier slighted.*

The people kicked against the cost of their protectors, and their rulers were hard put to it to scrape up the revenue needed for their maintenance. For the time being, civil law was in abeyance, and there ensued a struggle for survival amongst the independent princes and knights. Each strove to rectify his frontier at the expense of his neighbour, and the simplest expedient was found to be the occupation of a rival's territory with armed troops, in an entirely peaceable manner, for there was literally no possibility on either side of proceeding to the extremes of active hostilities. There was not sufficient vitality remaining to appeal to the final arbitrament of battle, for, on the first hint of such intention, the cattle would have disappeared again in the forests and the people have taken cover within their walled towns to make common cause against both forces.

A prince's revenue in those days depended principally upon the numbers of his people. The addition of a million souls practically meant so much more to his rent-roll, and, the cost of an Army remaining relatively a fixed quantity, an augmentation of territory rendered it possible either to lighten the taxation of his original subjects or to save up more money to pay for additional troops.

The latter course was that most usually favoured—because there being no field for the profitable investment of capital in banks, or industries, etc.—the best-paying investments were trained and armed men who could be employed in settling disputes about land with one's neighbour.

But this employment of troops needed enormous tact in its application, for it was not only necessary, as pointed out above, to prevent the civil population turning against both sides, but it was also most desirable to make it apparent to the inhabitants of the occupied territory, that life under the protection of King Log was preferable to their previous existence under King Stork. Hence arose, not only the need for rigid discipline within the armies themselves, but for the most extreme consideration for the rights and property of individuals;

because, if actual war resulted, supplies would immediately disappear unless the conduct of the troops beforehand had been so excellent that the country people continued willing to bring their cattle and food to the marketplaces. It was also found that everywhere ready-money payments proved the best commissariat officers.

It is necessary to insist on this point because, without a tolerably complete knowledge of all that it entails, it is impossible to understand the conditions which hampered all regular forces during the latter years of the eighteenth century, and alone rendered the strategy of the French Revolutionary forces practicable.

A few illustrations may serve to drive the lesson home. In 1785 the Austrian troops, being on the march against the Turks, the ferrymen on the Save struck for higher pay and the unfortunate commander had to write to Vienna for authority and the money to comply with their requirements.

During the Austrian occupation of the Netherlands, and whilst hostilities were actually raging with the French, the Austrian commanders were compelled not only to pay ready money for all supplies but to pay rent for their camping grounds and soldiers' quarters, and when this rent was not forthcoming, for some sick and wounded left behind on the line of march, the miserable men were thrown out into the streets, and would have perished but for the humanity of the Catholic priests and their institutions. Finally, in 1793, during the siege of Mayence, when the French were actually entering the city, a battalion of Austrian infantry could find no boatmen to take them across the river to Kastel, because the officer commanding had unfortunately no money in his pocket for their fares, and the boatmen insisted on payment in advance. The battalion accordingly laid down its arms![2]

Practically, therefore, an Austrian, or indeed any, com-

2. For these and many similar instances see *Geist und Stoff*, by C. von B-K; and the *Mitheilungen aus-dem K, K. Archive*, Vols. IV. and V.

mander's hands, other than those in the French Army, were as much tied by custom and tradition as were our own during manoeuvres in England twenty years ago. The troops might be—indeed as units they were—admirable in smartness, drill and efficiency, but if the provision wagons did not arrive in time the men went supperless to sleep in the open. This was a condition of things for which the regular soldier of those days had not bargained, and if repeated too often he was apt to hold that it relieved him of his oath of allegiance, consequently he took the first opportunity of deserting.

So thoroughly indeed had the troops assimilated this teaching that the civil population in Central Europe had become almost indifferent to their presence. Trade went on in the same way whether their country was at peace or at war, and as long as this happened to be the case they cared little what colour of coat the soldiers about them might wear. Either fighting man was equally good for trade purposes, and would have been welcomed everywhere, but for the fatal havoc their uniforms and good temper wrought amongst the womenfolk. This the civilian never has been able to condone in any age, and it still forms the root evil from which Continental socialism has sprung in almost every instance. Again this particular condition of affairs must be seriously grasped, as otherwise it is impossible to account for the general apathy with which the French invasion of southern Germany was so long regarded, and for the failure of the inhabitants to assist, even by information, the Austrians who in 1805 at least might reasonably have been accepted not only as compatriots but as deliverers.

It is difficult for us in these days of intensified nationalism to assign their full value to these many hindrances to an active strategy, and the sneer at a commander's lethargy is apt to spring too readily to our lips. But, in fairness to the generals who bore the brunt and burden of those anxious days, the attempt to understand these difficulties should be made before we venture to criticise them, and I would most earnestly impress upon everyone who wishes to deduce useful lessons for his own guidance from the study of the French—and in particular the Napoleonic—campaigns, to saturate his mind thoroughly with the civil history of the period first of all. Then he will be able to picture the difficulties with which Napoleon's opponents were compelled to grapple. We did not appreciate the criticisms so freely lavished on us for our slowness and apparent incapacity during the Boer War. Let us at least not fall into the same error of judgment when trying to understand the evolution of other armies.

To resume, all these factors acted and reacted on one another to cause difficulties in supply, which in turn developed slowness in the execution of strategical designs, which again of necessity developed a predilection on the part of the higher commands for the tactical defensive, and unfortunately the whole evolution of the fighting spirit of the Army had tended in the same direction. Generally the defensive had been forced upon them by their long struggle against the aggression of the Turks, but more particularly by the closing years of the Seven Years' War, in which, time and again, as at Hochkirch, Torgau, and many lesser encounters, the older officers, and even many of the men still serving at the outbreak of the Revolutionary wars, had seen the Prussian infantry hurl themselves recklessly upon their abattis and field entrenchments only to be beaten back with most crushing punishment. With these concrete lessons before their eyes the younger generation lost sight altogether of the deeper conditions which alone had enabled them to find time for this preparation of their positions.

As long as Frederick the Great had only the Austrians to deal with, his rapid manoeuvres never gave them time for serious entrenchment, but when Russia joined the Austrians and each maintained an Army numerically equivalent to the Prussian, the time the latter spent in marching from enemy to enemy, could be utilised by the one not immediately under fire to dig itself in to the eyes behind earthworks and obstacles which the shell power of those days was quite inadequate to cope with. The results of the desperate assaults delivered by the Prussians remained burnt in upon the brains of the Allies whilst the deeper causes, which alone had rendered their positions impregnable, never appealed to their imaginations at all. The older men, who did in fact know the cause and sequence of events, had died out long before the French wars began, and the younger ones, those who had been subalterns during the great campaigns, now took the field thoroughly saturated with the fundamental theory of the defensive.

It is difficult to make clear in a few words the terrible consequences that ensue when once this idea becomes dominant in a mass of men. When ordered to attack, instead of feeling within themselves the sense of the irresistible fury of their onslaught, each sees in imagination his opposite number on the enemy's side comfortably behind his parapet, and thinks how easily he himself, if the situation were reversed, could shoot the other down. He cannot visualise the actual reality opposed to him *viz.* the bullet-swept trench, choked with dead and wounded, the consequence of some unseen enfilading fire skilfully contrived by his own commander, and from which the survivors are furtively slipping under cover of the smoke and dust while the commander himself has no time to send down short tactical essays on the situation, to be read at the head of each company before it advances. The whole line hesitates, moves forward a few paces, then the thought-wave of the crowd overpowers the resolution of the individual, and the whole crowd halts, blazes aimlessly away towards their enemy, and no power on earth except fresh reinforcements will suffice to drive it forward again. Meanwhile the enemy in turn brings up his reinforcements and, if at last a forward impulse is secured, the opportunity has passed, and the denser line meets with double and treble the punishment it would have encountered had it obeyed more promptly. "The longer you are out in the rain, the wetter you get."

So it is now, and so it was then for death is the ultimate factor, and the distance at which it meets a man matters nothing.

Success in the attack rests on a mutual contract between the men and their leader in which in effect the latter says: "Obey my orders implicitly and I will place you in such a position relatively to your enemy that you cannot fail to beat him," and if he is a man of experience, and has again and again led them to victory never giving them a task beyond their power to perform the men give him their obedience readily, and will spring forward with alacrity to seize the opportunity they know that his skill and judgment have already secured for them. Under such a leader an Army soon becomes irresistible. But in an Army which has never experienced the joy of victory, with its logical corollary of pursuit, but only the tempered satisfaction of having escaped annihilation, things go from bad to worse. This is particularly the case with troops in which the esprit de corps is concentrated in the regimental unit. The defence fails generally only at a single point, and through this gap the enemy pour in, outflanking in succession all the remaining elements of the line, most of whom, having ample warning, get away in good order colours flying and ranks well closed. When later, round the camp fires, praise and blame are duly apportioned everyone agrees that but for the disgraceful conduct of the regiment such misfortune would never have arisen, but that the disgrace is amply made up for by the admirable courage with which the remainder made good their retreat; and since there are usually but few survivors of the left to contest this verdict it passes into tradition, and no one looks further for a deeper cause of the debacle. But in an Army with many regiments it takes time to ring all the changes and give to each its turn, hence if now and again victory shines locally on a regiment here and there, years may elapse before the inherent weakness of the whole organisation is exposed. This, in fact, is what actually happened to the Austrian regiments in the years from 1793 to 1805. Though generally unsuccessful in the greater battles, they were as constantly successful in "not getting beaten" in small commands; and even after Marengo the confidence of the regimental leaders in their methods and their men was very far from being thoroughly shaken.

Not that there were wanting, as in every Army, hundreds of would-be reformers ready to reform everything from the standpoint of the individual soldier and the advantages of an intact skin. But these destructionists, though sufficiently numerous to cause an ill-defined feeling of inferiority to the French throughout the Austrian mass, were still powerless to induce the responsible commanders to introduce a root-and-branch reconstruction such as that which the Prussian Army underwent after 1806, and those responsible were right to hold their hands, for the passions of the people were as yet not nearly sufficiently aroused to supply the driving force which the French methods required.[3]

We must therefore picture the Austrian Army as a number of units, faultlessly turned out, slow, precise and methodic perfect to take advantage of a tactical situation that gave them suitable targets against which to develop their fire power, but so hampered by conditions beyond the direct control of their leaders that, in practice, the latter were never able to contrive the strategic situations which would have justified the traditional tactical methods.

Since then this has been precisely paralleled in South Africa. The British regular troops were at least as superior to the Boer commandos, as fighting units, as were the Austrians to the first French levies and with equal mobility our men would have swept their opponents off the field, as both Austrians, Prussians and British had exterminated the French when they were fortunate enough to catch them in positions which gave the advantage to the inherent power of coher-

3. Yorck's Landwehr at Wartenburg and at Mockern (1813). See Campaign, "Leipzig" (by the Author).

ent action, which is the birthright of regular troops; but as in 1793 so in South Africa, the absence of mobility, due to causes far beyond the control of our executive commanders, never allowed us the chance of demonstrating once for all the fundamental difference between an army and a rabble, however brave and skilful the individuals composing the latter might happen to be.

But the Austrian commanders laboured under yet another disadvantage from which, in 1899, we were at least free. Not only were they fighting some 800 miles away from their original base (and 800 miles of land transport over the roads then existing was a more serious hindrance than 10,000 miles of rail and sea), but they were immeasurably more at the mercy of fraudulent contractors than we perhaps have ever been, and from the nature of their organisation they were less able to protect themselves from this most pernicious scourge than were other Western armies. Their Army being officered exclusively from the Austrian aristocracy and the rank and file drawn from the country, there was no middle class of men available to officer the Train and Supply Service generally and thus to stand between the men and the contractor. This is always and everywhere a problem most difficult of solution, for the men of birth naturally strive to get forward into the fighting line and men promoted for Train service from the ranks of an Army recruited almost exclusively from the peasantry, have neither education nor imagination enough to cope with the wiles of the contractor.

The cause of the corruption which hitherto has always prevailed in the rear of the fighting line is not, as is usually assumed, the innate wickedness of individuals who care nothing for the lives of their comrades at the front if only their own pockets are sufficiently well lined (though a few such men no doubt are always to be found), it is far rather due to the sum of infinitesimal lapses from the letter of the law, brought about by that form of careless and stupid good-nature, that fails to trace the connection between cause and effect. The individual sees no harm in accepting a drink for overlooking some minor irregularity seemingly unimportant in itself, but when millions of such irregularities are allowed to pass unnoticed the cumulative effect at the front becomes disastrous.

In this respect the Austrians were in worse case than either the French or Prussian armies. The former, having little, if any, organised Supply Service, dealt with the peasant direct, through the medium of the stick; and in the latter the spirit of duty, the outcome of the Thirty Years' War, had taken far firmer root than amongst the more genial and care-free inhabitants of the south, the bulk of whom had in fact escaped the ravages of that most calamitous struggle. Hence it followed that everywhere beyond the immediate ken of the combatant Austrian officers at the front hospitals and sick wards were crowded with uncared-for cripples and invalids. Moreover, diseases due to unsanitary conditions were chronic, and reinforcements, half starved already by neglect of the commissariat, fell victims by thousands on their way to the front, whilst the survivors often required weeks of nursing before they were really fit for the ranks.

Under these conditions and limitations the Austrian strategical methods slowly developed themselves. Being strictly tied to their heavy supply columns they could only march by good roads, and such roads being few in number it followed that they advanced on a broad front, needing many hours to close in to a line of battle. Between the gaps which thus arose, the lightly equipped independent French levies poured in, attacking individual columns like hornets, and thus breaking down all the elaborate time calculations of the Austrian Staff, which were as ingenious in design as were our own recent efforts to entrap de Wet and his comrades in South Africa.

As the disciplined Austrian soldiery simply despised the *sans-culotte* rabble, and when on the defensive felt themselves a match for any odds, the columns on the roads diminished in strength, and the men thus made available were sent out to guard the flanks, till, when a general action did at last ensue, the proportion of muskets available per yard of front sank almost as low as in some of our own engagements in recent years. Thus at Stokach in 1800 the Austrians with some 25,000 combatants held a line at least thirty miles long, and this is typical of many similar engagements. Indeed, until Napoleon appeared on the scene, local conditions compelled the French to adhere to a similar rule of dispersion. It was in planning these simultaneous deployments of many small columns over a very long front that Mack and Weyreuther, together with many more fortunate Staff companions, attained the heights of virtuosity, and this brings us to the evolution of the man whose reputation has so long suffered in the shadow of misfortune.

Few characters could be more difficult to portray, and it will be best to let the facts speak for themselves before attempting to appraise him.

Karl Mack was born on the 25th August 1752 at Neunslingen, in Bavaria. His father was a minor official and a Protestant, consequently he was as devoid of powerful protection as a man could well be. An uncle on his mother's side, Rittmeister Leiberich of the 2nd Carabiniers, took Karl back with him to his regiment, and in that he enlisted on the 16th January 1770, at the age of eighteen. His rise was by no means rapid; he got his first stripe on 1st May 1771, and on the 1st July 1773 became regimental adjutant a rank for which we have no exact equivalent but of far less importance than our modern sergeant-major—chief orderly-room clerk would be nearer the mark. Not till 1st April 1777 did he obtain his first commission, but then his progress became more rapid, for in February 1778 Field-Marshal Graf Lacy, Honorary Colonel of the 2nd Carabiniers, sent to the regiment for a smart young officer, a good writer and draughtsman, to accompany him and the Emperor Joseph in an inspection of the Bohemian frontiers which they were undertaking in view of strained relations with Prussia. Mack was selected and had to note down all the remarks made by the Emperor during the day's march, and read them out in the evening, adding the Field-Marshal's comments, and then enter them up in a special journal. On the outbreak of hostilities later in the year, Lacy retained Mack as secretary, and on the 8th July 1778 he was promoted First Lieutenant, and returned to his regiment, whence he was transferred to the Q.M.G.'s department as Captain on the 3rd November 1783.

He was now employed in the Emperor's military cabinet, accompanying him in his annual inspection, winning Lacy's esteem and praise for his ceaseless energy and devotion to duty. In 1786, in view of the war then pending with the Turks, he was transferred to the Hungarian command, and served with headquarters throughout the following campaign. Most of the mobilisation work was done by him, and he was warmly praised by the Emperor, Lacy, Hadik and Kinsky, receiving as his reward promotion to Major, 24th May 1788, and the appointment of A.D.C. to the Emperor.

On the 25th January 1789 he was made Lieutenant-Colonel, and for a time his luck appeared to change, for F.M. Loudon, who took over the command in July 1789, received him coldly. Mack asked to be transferred, stating that he felt he could not do useful work unless fully trusted. The straightforwardness of his attack, and manner of making it, so pleased the Field-Marshal that he took him into favour for the time being. But fresh trouble arose when Mack vehemently urged upon his Chief to attack Belgrade, and refused to transmit Loudon's objections to the Kaiser. For this he was severely reprimanded. But he soon regained his former position and on the 19th October 1789 was made Colonel, receiving the much-coveted Maria Theresa Order. At the close of the year he returned with Loudon to Vienna and was employed on the mobilisation plans against Prussia; but his health had suffered so severely during the campaign that he was compelled to resign his appointment on the personal staff of the Emperor, and to take a prolonged furlough. He was quite unable to sit a horse, or to write, except lying down. However, he appears to have made at least a partial recovery, for in December 1790 he was given the command of the 3rd Chevaux Legers, but he remained during the winter in Vienna and lectured to the Archdukes Charles and Josef, winning the friendship and esteem of the former, which he retained for the next ten years.

In 1791 he rejoined his regiment and was with it when the war against the French Revolution broke out in April 1792. The command of the Field Army was at first given to F.M. the Duke of Sachsen-Teschen, but he was relieved the following year by F.M. Prince Josias of Sachsen-Coburg, whose name is still remembered in the British army as the General to whom the well-known cavalry inspection *march Die Coburger* was dedicated. The Prince begged for Mack as his Q.M.G., and Mack went with him under protest as he was still suffering from the illness contracted in the Turkish campaign.

The immediate object of the campaign was the relief of Maestricht. The two opposing forces were still in winter quarters and since secrecy was of the first importance the Prince remained in Coblentz, sending Mack on to the front to concert measures with Clerfayt, the temporary commander of the Austrian forces. Clerfayt was most averse to the idea of an immediate advance, as he wished to wait for reinforcements, but Mack by his energy overcame all his objections, winning for himself thereby the unstinted praise of Graf Tauenzien, the Prussian Military Commissioner with the Austrian headquarters, and in due course arrangements were made to force the passage of the Roer, which were brilliantly carried through on the 1st March 1793.

With reference to this operation Mack subsequently wrote:

The man who despises his enemy is a fool; the man who fears him a shirker. I could not see in these new republican Frenchmen the heroes of antiquity that many of my comrades saw. I did not believe that all their gunners were young Jupiters, throwing their thunderbolts with unerring aim, and I did not compare their numbers to the sands of the sea. Since after due reflection I concluded it would be cowardly to fear them, I advised the Prince indeed I implored him to attack, and thus arose this 1st March which surely deserves to be numbered in the list of eventful days.

As already mentioned, the attack succeeded, and during the next few days Maestricht was relieved and the French driven back behind Louvain. Writing to the Emperor, the Archduke Charles said: "It is to Colonel Mack that we all owe our thanks he has distinguished himself everywhere by his energy, ability and courage," testimony which he again repeated in a second letter dated a few days later; and two years later, when Mack himself wrote to Coburg to congratulate the Prince on the anniversary of the battle the latter replied in the following very remarkable terms:

No; the 1st March is your day. It is you we have to thank that the line of the Roer was not abandoned. It was thanks to you that the decision was come to, to cross the river. You alone drew up and carried out the admirable dispositions for the operation which remain a model for all time. In fact but for you the opinion of others, who held the enemy's position as unassailable, would have prevailed, and we should have retired with nothing accomplished.

Surely higher testimony as to Mack's value at the time could hardly be desired.

Political influences of the usual nature now arrested the

Austrian advance, and the French, having rallied, were led back to the attack by Dumouriez on the 18th March. There ensued the battle of Neerwinden, a long and indecisive struggle very characteristic of the period. The right wing of the Austrians gained some slight advantage, but the left, under Clerfayt, only with difficulty held its own. In the middle of the afternoon Mack collapsed completely under one of his attacks of illness and was carried into a neighbouring house. Here during the course of the evening he was found by Coburg, who came to tell him of the decision arrived at in his absence, to retreat. This news stung Mack back into sudden life. With all his energy he urged the Prince to attack again immediately, and that night, or in the early morning, Coburg consented, and rode off to give the orders. But Clerfayt in particular brought forward such strong grounds for inaction it is always so easy to find them that the Prince once more hesitated and rode back to Mack to announce his fresh intention to retreat. Mack was now thoroughly roused. He urged the Prince "for God's sake don't think of retreat, it would be a disgrace," and poured forth such a torrent of speech that the group of waverers again hesitated, and finally, the Archduke Charles strongly supporting Mack, it was decided to act on the offensive at dawn. Long before the appointed time Mack pulled himself together and was lifted on to his horse by two orderlies and rode out to supervise the proceedings. Reaching the rendezvous, where the troops were already forming up, he learnt from the returning patrols that the enemy had already decamped.

Again political influences intervened to prevent an immediate pursuit. Then followed the fatal negotiations with Dumouriez, in which Mack went far beyond his instructions, and both he and his Commander were not only severely reprimanded, but experienced the added misfortune of incurring the enmity of the Minister Thugut, who was just then beginning to make his name.

No rewards were given to the Army and, naturally enough under the circumstances, none to Mack. But the Archduke Charles took up their common cause, and in a letter to the Kaiser pleaded for Mack with all his force. After pointing out the succession of advantages secured by the discipline and endurance of the troops, he continued:

> . . . . but all this good work must be attributed to Mack who, suffering most pitifully from ill health, gave himself with all his remaining energy to the cause, working literally day and night. In short, the whole Army loves and honours him and looks up to him as the originator of all its victories.

The Prince himself had recommended Mack for promotion after Neerwinden, and in a subsequent letter to the Emperor he wrote:

> If the services of this officer are overlooked it will have a most serious effect on the spirit of the Army, while he will feel himself humiliated, and will probably resign.

On receipt of this the Emperor accorded Mack a money grant and promised further promotion in due course; but it never came and Mack, worn out by illness, as well as deeply hurt at this neglect, asked to be relieved of his appointment. Coburg too was so annoyed that he also asked to be allowed to resign, and again applied for Mack's promotion in the name of the whole Army. A letter from Graf Mercy, who was attached to the Prince in a diplomatic capacity, was also written in support of Mack:

> I have never in my life seen Herr von Mack, but I gathered at once on my arrival that he was the life and soul of all the military operations; that he possesses the confidence of the whole Army, and that it would be difficult to replace him.

Whilst this correspondence was still in progress Mack himself was wounded somewhat severely in the battle of Famars (23rd and 24th May 1793), the plan for which engagement he had drawn up. Thus his return on sick leave became imperative. The Emperor gave him the colonelcy of the Cuirassier Regiment Jacquemin but still no step in rank.

In June he was sufficiently recovered to travel, and passing through Vienna went back to a small property he had recently acquired near Iglau.

It would seem that his well-known friendship with Lacy was the underlying cause of his many disappointments. Lacy had always been against the War, and had never underrated the strength of the French resistance; but the heads of the Army throughout all this time were purposely kept in ignorance of the secret aims of the Imperial policy by Thugut, who did not want to win the Netherlands by fighting, but wished to make the other parties to the alliance pull the chestnuts out of the fire for Austria's benefit; and of course Mack's vigorous fighting policy, in which he was encouraged by Lacy, proved sadly disconcerting to his designs.

Meanwhile Hohenlohe had replaced Coburg at the front, and a series of disasters set in. On the 4th January 1794 the Archduke Charles again wrote to the Emperor:

> Since Mack has left us all has gone wrong. . . . I can tell you much more when we meet. If only you were here and could see for yourself. Even the Hungarian Grenadiers say that things have gone from bad to worse since they no longer see 'the man with the white mantle' riding about amongst them. If Mack were fit to serve and perhaps he will be ere this reaches you he is above all the man for the Q.M. Generalship of this command. The whole Army agrees in this, and longs for his return and it would be well to build a 'golden bridge' to induce him to accept the post and come back to us.

Actually before this letter arrived, the golden bridge had already been built, but it took some trouble to get Mack to cross it, for he declined at first altogether, and only consented when he learnt that the Emperor was going to the front in person. Assured of this he lost no time in returning to Vienna, which he reached on the 26th December 1793. He at once proceeded to urge a most vigorous forward policy on the Cabinet, dwelling particularly on the need of retaining Prussian support, and in all this he was fully backed up by Lacy and the principal military authorities. But so tortuous was the policy of the Cabinet under Thugut that he was allowed to leave for the front without any knowledge of the fact that, in consequence of the partition of Poland, the Prussian Alliance was not only already at an end, but Prussia was actually inclining towards an agreement with France.

In January 1794 he reached Brussels, where he was received "as a Messiah," and at a conference held on the 4th February, at which the Archduke Charles, the Duke of Coburg, Duke of York, Crown Prince of Orange, Graf Mercy and the British Ambassador Lord Elgin, were present, the plan of campaign for the coming year was decided upon. Essentially it was all Mack's work, but the details need not delay us. He urged a vigorous offensive and demanded 340,000 men, of whom 140,000 were to be left on the Rhine the remaining 200,000 were to attack the Netherlands. But to raise this number needed the cooperation of all the Allies, and even now he seems to have been unaware that Prussia had decided to withdraw her contingent. For himself, he immediately started for London where he was most cordially received. The King presented him with a jewelled sword of honour, and laden with promises of support he returned to the Netherlands on the 19th February, and rode down his line of outposts to Trier, where he expected to find his final instructions. These, however, had not arrived, and in an evil moment he stepped outside his purely military duties and undertook negotiations with the enemy direct. This gave Thugut and his party the handle they needed. His recall was decided on, but while Thugut was in Vienna the Emperor was with headquarters, and, whilst letters were on the road, Mack had so firmly ingratiated himself with his sovereign that his position for the moment was unassailable.

The opening of the campaign, in spite of the withdrawal of the Prussians, was all in his favour, but again he found himself confronted with a web of intrigue, his health once more broke down, and utterly worn out he at length belied his whole previous record by counselling retreat unless another 40,000 men could be guaranteed him at once. So great was his ascendancy though still only Quartermaster-General that it was felt necessary to secure his removal in some way, and since Mack would not serve except under the eyes of the Emperor, reasons had to be given which made the return of the Monarch to the capital unavoidable, and unsuspiciously Mack went with him. Thugut and his friends naturally attributed all the misfortunes of the war to Mack, but this was manifestly so unjust that all his soldier friends rallied round him, and the British at the front clamoured to have him back again. Coburg himself begged him to return, or at least to send him advice. But Mack for the time being was too ill for service anywhere, and remained in retirement until the middle of 1796.

Bonaparte's progress in Italy, however, called him into action again, and it was proposed to send him as Staff Officer to the Archduke Charles, but Thugut defeated this proposition and tried to get him to accept the command of the Portuguese Army which had been offered him. This Mack declined with thanks, and he was then made Chief of the Staff to the Army of the Interior, and in this capacity was called on for his advice on all possible points. This brought him into collision with the Archduke Charles and thus the long friendship between the two was undermined. In the summer of 1798, at the particular request of Queen Caroline of Naples, backed by the Emperor himself, he accepted the command of the Neapolitan Army and joined at Caserta on the 9th October 1778. Here he was received with open arms and seemed to have won the Army at first sight. Even Nelson, who at first was inclined to think little of him, became a convert in a few days, and cordially praised his activity and general capacity. But Mack failed to comprehend the Neapolitan character; deceived by the smart appearance of the men on parade—they were said to be the best turned-out troops in Europe—he allowed himself to be goaded into a premature advance against Championnet, and having designed a manoeuvre in five columns (well within the capacity of his old Netherland veterans) he had the mortification to witness the hopeless collapse of his Army, which turned upon him and ultimately compelled him to seek safety in the lines of his enemy. General Championnet received him with all honour and gave him a safe-conduct back to his own country, but he was arrested by Bonaparte's order in Bologna, and taken to Paris, whence, after many attempts to secure an exchange, he escaped in disguise and reached Austrian territory in safety in April 1800. Again Thugut's animosity defeated its own object. Clearly Mack was not to blame for the gross misconduct of his command, and when, in January 1801, Thugut's ministry came to an end the way was open to Mack's re-employment, but, as the sequel will show, this soon brought him into collision with the Archduke Charles for the second time. Here for the moment we will leave him, only asking the reader to focus his attention on the salient points of Mack's character his unexampled rise from obscurity; the singular strength of affection and esteem he succeeded in inspiring in his commanding officers, all of whom were of the highest aristocracy; and the devotion of his troops; his great personal courage, and his devouring energy and determination, which only faltered once, under a weight of suffering both mental and physical that would have killed a weaker man. In his defence I shall have more to say in the final summing-up of the campaign; meanwhile it will be sufficient to beg the reader to preserve an attitude of impartial and suspended judgment, until the final chapters of this most remarkable career have been laid before him.

Taking now the three arms and their accessories more in detail, the chief strength of the Austrian Army lay in its Light Infantry, which in fact had always been the model for the rest of Western Europe. Recruited primarily amongst the frontier races and reinforced by selected men from the more regular provinces, they had been trained by generations of warfare with the Turks, and had proved their superiority against Christian opponents, more especially during the Seven Years' War. In fact they may claim to have given the original impetus to the transformation of all infantry into individual fighters, for it was to meet them that in 1792 the French raised their first regular battalions of Voltigeurs, whose example ultimately dominated the trend of French infantry tactics, which in turn set the example for the modern German school. The French were, of course, helped in this process of transmutation by the numbers of their soldiers who had returned from the great struggle for dominion in Canada and the United States, but had it not been for the necessity forced upon them by the Austrian light infantry the old school of the Line tacticians would hardly have been so rapidly and so thoroughly converted. Their regulations would stand almost without modification even at the present day, and they were not only letter-perfect in their knowledge of them, but they retained the real Light Infantry spirit, without which regulations, however perfect, are of little or no avail.

The regular infantry was modelled almost entirely on the same lines as the Prussian, but, as already pointed out, it lacked the offensive spirit characteristic of the latter, and probably for that very reason never attempted to emulate its prototype in rapidity of fire: for defence rests essentially on accuracy of fire, whilst the success of an attack has always been determined by the weight of metal thrown in a given time. It is not so much the object of the assailant to hit his adversary, but rather to create such conditions smoke, dust, bullets and so forth as shall make it difficult or impossible for the covered antagonist to take adequate aim, and this holds good whatever the nature of the weapons employed.

Its regimental Transport was also, as in Prussia, carefully organised, and each regiment or battalion could be readily detached for independent operations.

The Cavalry also had endeavoured to imitate their former adversaries; but here, too, the "Man," on whom in the long run cavalry efficiency invariably depends, had not been found to bring home to all ranks the simple bed-rock principles on which the success of the charge of a cavalry mass always ultimately hinges, and to teach them to deliver a knee-to-knee charge in two clear and well-defined ranks; for in 1789 we find Mack reporting that there were few, if any, squadrons which could gallop a couple of hundred yards without falling into confusion, and on such points Mack could speak with full authority. Actually, in spite of its immense superiority in numbers and material over its opponents, in the wars of the Revolution, it achieved nothing worthy of special mention, even when large bodies fifty squadrons and upwards were available for employment on the field.

The Artillery, also as a consequence of the trend of events during the latter portion of the Seven Years' War, was relatively wanting in mobility, and, as M. Colin and other French authorities have shown, was handicapped by a gun, weight for weight intrinsically inferior to that in use in the French Army. Though the change from battalion guns to batteries had commenced during the Italian campaign, the spirit of the change had not really got hold of the arm, and the true Battery Commander had yet to be created—precisely as was the case in England at the same time.

The most serious defect of the whole Army, however, lay in

the want of organised units higher than the regiment or battalion. Though in time of war it had always been the custom, as in other armies, to form detachments of all arms for special purposes, the units of which they were composed retained their organic independence, and were, so to speak, only lent to the detachment Commander by Army headquarters for temporary tactical purposes, resuming their place in the Army as a whole when this temporary connection was brought to a close. The idea of decentralisation, in fact, had not even begun to dawn upon the Austrian Staff, and though bodies of troops might fight as brigades, and even divisions, Field Army headquarters still sent out orders in detail to each unit in the command. The evil of superfluous correspondence which this involved had long been felt, but the only idea that presented itself to the harassed detachment Commanders to minimise it appears to have been the assignment of more clerical assistance to their headquarters, not, as in France, the elimination of the evil itself by adequate methods of delegation of responsibility. Thus in the Prince of Hohenzollern's diary of the Marengo campaign, published about 1896 by the Austrian General Staff,[4] we find Generals writing to Vienna complaining of their endless copying tasks and petitioning for more clerks to be sent for their assistance. Later, we shall find Mack justifying the delay in the issue of orders that was the primary cause of the defeat of Elchingen on the ground that his operation orders necessitated the writing of fourteen sheets of foolscap in which "there was not one superfluous word."

Fundamentally this was the essential cause of all Austrian defeats during the Revolutionary wars and indeed for long afterwards. The French owed their successes primarily to superior mobility, but there is no reason to suppose that the well drilled, long-service battalions of Austria were actually slower marchers than their opponents indeed, the contrary

4. The book has been lost from the library I have been using, hence I am unable to give the exact reference. The date, however, will be sufficient guidance,

would seem to be the more reasonable supposition, and there is some evidence to prove it. *The real cause lay in the hopeless over-centralisation of affairs in the Field headquarters, which rendered it impossible to get out orders in time to meet a sudden emergency.*

Such a want of system paralysed the individual efforts of even the best Staff Officers, and judged by contemporary standards the Austrian Staff actually were very highly trained. On paper, their curriculum would compare very favourably indeed with that of our own Staff College not twenty years ago. There is ample proof of the zeal and industry with which they threw themselves into their work, and the appalling intricacy of the detail and methods which they succeeded in committing to memory; *but in War, time is always the essence of the contract*, and no amount of science can reduce the actual time limit required to copy so and so many sheets of paper and despatch them by orderlies on dark nights over rough and often unknown country.

A final cause of inferiority inherent in the Austrian Army, as compared with the French, lay in the fact that from the nature of the whole Austrian constitution it was impossible—practically speaking—for the Sovereign to accompany his Armies in the field, hence all questions involving the policy of the State as a whole had to be referred to the Chancellery in Vienna for decision. Now since these were constantly arising, owing to the multiplicity of interests, of Allies, of dependencies, etc., involved in the very wide sphere of operations, it was impossible to give the Commanders of Armies and detachments the free hand that is so essential for immediate decisions. Hence the necessity of the "Hofkriegsrath" to which we generally give the name of the "Aulic Council." This body has earned an evil notoriety, which, in fact, it scarcely seems to have deserved, for having once laid down the objects for which each Command was to work, it forbore altogether to tie the hands of the Commander as to the employment of the means given into his hand for the specific purpose.

The real fault lay in this, that owing to the length of the lines of communication, as measured by time and space, the relative importance of the objects indicated had often changed altogether before the Army had reached its destination. Hence constant cross-references, out of which arose the habit of postponing decisions, which culminated in a positive disease of irresolution in all ranks, both on the march and in actual presence of the enemy.[5]

To sum up the whole situation, the Austrian Army from 1792 to 1805 was superior at every point but one to its enemy, and proved itself to be so when, during the Italian campaign of 1799, this one point, this fatal vice of irresolution in its commanders, was temporarily removed by the extraordinary personal magnetism of Suvaroff. But once this influence was withdrawn the fatal habit again reasserted itself, and the conservative spirit inherent in the bulk of the Army its self-respect again restored by the succession of victories it had won under his command asserted itself again, and fatally hampered the efforts towards rational reform which men like Mack, and others, attempted to introduce.

5. Actually the worst interference with the action of commanders in the field is to be traced to the influence of one man—the minister Thugut—and this particularly in the case of Suvaroff in Italy, 1799. *Vide Geist und Stoff.*

Chapter 2
The French Army

During the past century, practically all strategical discussion has turned on the question of numbers essentially numbers, whether they were enumerated by battalions, squadrons and batteries or merely by men only the assumption always being that 150,000 men would beat 100,000 under whatever conditions the two forces might encounter one another.

It is curious to notice that in the previous century no such significance was attached to the question of numerical superiority at all, efficiency of the units being assigned a far more important place. If the skill of the leader and the manoeuvring power of the units he commanded rendered it possible for him to throw his whole force against a salient or flank of his enemy, the question of numbers mattered very little indeed. In fact the smaller army had the advantage, because, its internal resistance being less, it could manoeuvre faster and with greater certainty. The problem the generals of the French Revolutionary Army had to solve in face of the enemy was to find some means by which the advantage of superior efficiency could be neutralised and the brute force of sheer numbers be given a fuller scope. The full solution was not arrived at until the new Army, after many disastrous experiences, had evolved a leader free from all traditions of the past, the very personification of the relentless spirit of the whole nation which the French Revolution had evolved.

It was the spirit of the French nation primarily which conditioned the whole growth and development of Napoleon's methods, both strategical and tactical, and without a firm grasp of this fundamental proposition the study of his campaigns will always remain a barren expenditure of energy.

The steps in this evolution were threefold. In the first place, the French nation being caught in almost defenceless condition, its representatives were compelled to get back to the very bed-rock conditions of primitive warfare, and, as far as lay in their power, to compel every man, woman and child to contribute at least its share of uncomplaining endurance to the national defence.

One may smile at the inflated bombast of the many proclamations issued, but the spirit of defence *a outrance* breathed in them, and they reflected sufficiently the great psychologic wave of emotion which swept over France and enabled individuals to endure hardship and tyranny many times worse than anything they had experienced in the past. I have said "individuals" because it is necessary to keep the sequence of cause and effect clearly before one's mind.

The wave of emotion swept over fully two-thirds of the race, and made everyone realise very fully the absolute obligation laid upon his neighbour to die for the State. But in the beginning it was only individuals who responded personally to this national demand, and not till the new Army had evolved its own soul did the men in the actual fighting line become other than volunteers.

The old Army with its traditions amalgamated the new levies, receiving in the process a new spirit. Subsequently, when the new Army had acquired solidity and traditions of its own, it became strong enough to assimilate even unwilling conscripts and induce them to fight with loyalty and spirit for their leader and the cause he embodied, which after all they felt to be the cause of their country first.

Previously to the outbreak of the Revolution, the Royal Army of France had been identical with the royal armies of all other Western kingdoms, a body of long-service mercenaries representing only a small fraction of the nation, and living as a caste apart. But during the fifty years of peace, or relative peace, that had followed after Roszbach, being strictly localised, they had gradually fused with the civilians and developed the sentiment of nationality, side by side with that of loyalty to their salt. When the break came, by far the larger half of those remaining with the colours elected to side with the nation, and the nucleus thus left proved in fact sufficient to assimilate the successive drafts of volunteers and conscripts which the nation subsequently brooded. During the first years of the War the Regular Army was recruited side by side with the Volunteers, and never fought with more than fifty per-cent, of recruits in the ranks. In the first instance men came forward far more readily for the Volunteer battalions, but as these latter melted away for want of proper officers to feed and care for them at the front, the best of them, seeing the advantages of belonging to a real regimental family, joined the regulars and brought with them that individual knowledge of the advantages of discipline which no one appreciates better than the man who has suffered the consequences which its absence invariably entails.

The final fusion, the "Amalgam" it was called, between the Line and the Volunteers thus came about quite naturally as the survival of the fittest; the Volunteers were tired of the licence their relative liberty procured, and the Line were altogether sick of fighting shoulder to shoulder with battalions whose discipline could not be relied on.

At the outbreak of the Revolution the Army numbered 79 French and 23 Foreign Infantry Regiments; 12 battalions of Chasseurs, 7 Artillery Regiments, 26 Regiments of Heavy Cavalry, 18 Dragoons, 6 of Hussars, and 12 of Chasseurs á Cheval (Mounted Light Infantry), totalling in all 175,000 men. Behind them stood a Militia of 55,000 to 70,000 men, and, as a kind of reservoir upon which to draw, 2,571,700 National Guards, without any organisation or even arms, who in obedience to a proclamation had enrolled themselves voluntarily, to escape the danger of being forcibly pressed for the front. Here and there a few battalions had organised themselves to protect their own property from the violence of the mob. These organisations, according to Thiebault, became fairly efficient units, and formed useful schools of arms, from which later many good officers were derived.

A proposal to introduce a stringent law of compulsory service had been rejected by a large majority of the Chambers, as out of harmony with the principles for which the Revolution was contending; hence, when in 1791 the war clouds burst over it, the Government of the moment had to help itself by a series of expedients from day to day.

Though, as pointed out above, the Regiments as a whole stood firm in their allegiance to the country, each Regiment had to undergo a little revolution within itself to adapt itself to its new situation. Needless to say, these readjustments were not carried out without much suffering and many instances of personal hardships; yet about two thirds of the whole seem to have held together and formed a sufficiently strong nucleus to digest their new recruits.

These, however, were at first difficult to find. Instead of expanding existing "cadres" in a normal manner, the Assembly decreed in July, 1791, the formation of 169 Volunteer battalions, recruited from the enrolled National Guards. This decree was received with enthusiasm in Paris, and in a few days no less than three battalions were formed, but then the enthusiasm began to flicker out, and by September 25 only sixty were available for service, and very few of these appear to have reached the front. These men, however, were only called upon to serve for the "Campaign" which, according to the custom of the period, was held to terminate, quite irrespective of the enemy's ideas, on December 1; and as they also received while enrolled a higher rate of pay than the Line, the latter found themselves deprived of their supply of recruits and dwindled away visibly.

The confusion and want of discipline in this first levy were appalling. The generals at the front were loud in their denunciation of these armed bandits, who robbed the inhabitants of their own country, setting the worst kind of examples to the Regular troops, and they clamoured for their withdrawal and replacement by troops of the Line. But the Committee of Public Safety saw in their unanimity a subtle design against the Revolution. Instead of stemming the evil, they aggravated it by decreeing the formation of a further 45 battalions, additional to the original 169, only 60 of which were in actual existence (May 5, 1792), all of the 214 to be brought up to a strength of 800 men.

On June 1, 1792, the Regular Army numbered 178,000 men, of whom 90,000 stood in face of the enemy. Of the Volunteers there appear to have been altogether 84,000 under arms, but these were the best, who had resisted the temptations to desert, or having tried the remedy had found it worse than the disease and returned to the colours, resigned to make the best of things. But these numbers were entirely inadequate to confront the gathering hosts of the Coalition. On July 11 the celebrated declaration, *La patrie en danger*, was issued, which called upon all men of an age to bear arms to consider themselves "mobilised" and to choose from their own districts those men who were to march first against the enemy.

These men were not to be known as "Volunteers" but were designated "Federes" because the battalions in which they were to march had no longer any territorial connection. They were put together from several departments, and were destined to recruit the Line and the Volunteers already at the front, to complete those units most advanced in formation, etc. A number of "Free Companies" of Chasseurs were also to be formed.

The result, however, was disappointing. Up to September 20 this proclamation brought in only 60,000 men, of whom not half reached the front, barely sufficient to make good the ordinary wastage. Yet it was with troops formed under such dispiriting conditions that Dumouriez won the battle of Jemappes. And the reason is not far to seek: only the best had survived their ordeals and reached the front.

In face of this state of affairs, and the addition of Great Britain to the ranks of the enemy, the National Convention was compelled to abandon the idea of voluntary service. On February 20, 1793, it decreed a compulsory levy of 300,000 men, distributed over the several communes, each of which was to issue an appeal for men to make up its quota, and if in three days the number was incomplete, the balance was to be made good by recourse to the ballot urn.

All unmarried National Guards between the ages of eighteen and forty were held liable for service.

At the same time, to put an end to the friction which had existed between the soldiers of the Regular Army and the Volunteers, the old white coat was taken away from the former, and all alike were compelled to wear the dark blue of the National Guard. A new unit was instituted, the "demi-brigade," which consisted of a Regular battalion and one or two Volunteer battalions, both retaining their own special peculiarities, other than the colour of their coats.

Yet the French Army survived even this extraordinary measure, It was with troops brigaded together in this wise that Napoleon won his victories in Italy in 1796 for the order by which the final "amalgam," as it was called, of Line and Volunteers was put into execution during the course of the campaign. In fact it only reached the Army of Italy a few days before he assumed the command.

This, however, in anticipation, and in the meanwhile French recruiting had many vicissitudes to endure. The proclamation was meeting with little success, and when the news of Dumouriez's defeat at Neerwinden (March 18, 1793) was received, a perfect panic of terror seized the nation. The Committee of Public Safety was elected, and forthwith proceeded to most drastic steps. Decree after decree was issued, each wilder than the other, until, on March 23, Barere's suggestions became law[1] and hundreds of thousands of men were driven to arms and despatched towards the frontier.

The internal paralysation of France was now complete, for these men robbed and plundered wherever they appeared, and deserted by tens of thousands. In a few months the desolation of the country was so complete that absolutely no other refuge for a man remained, where he could be reasonably secure against denunciation and hunger, except at the front. Then the tide turned and the Army began to receive a healthier and better type of recruit, men who, having had their fill of freedom, recognised at last the value of discipline

---

1. The preamble of the celebrated decree of August 23, 1793, drawn up by Barere, is as follows: *Jusqu'au moment ou les ennemis auront été chasses du territoire de la République, tous les Français sont en réquisition permanente pour le service des armées Les jeunes gens iront au combat; les hommes maries forgeront les armes et transporteront les subsistances; les femmes feront des tentes, des habits, et serviront dans les hôpitaux; les enfants mettront le vieux lings en charpie; les vieillards se feront porter sur les places publiques pour exciter le courage des guerriers, la haine des rois et le dévouement de la République. Les maisons nationales seront convertis en casernes; la sol des caves sera lessive pour en extraire le salpêtre*, etc., etc., and articles 8, 9, laid down, *Nul ne pourra se faire remplacer dans le service pour lequel il sera requis; les fonctionnaires publics resteront a leur postes La Levte sera générale, les citoyens non maries ou veufs sans enfants de 18 a 25 marchèrent les première*, but nothing is said as to when they return. Assuming, however, that the population of France at that date was in round numbers 30,000,000, then the annual contingent would be 300,000 men, of whom 200,000 would be physically fit to bear arms. If the duration of service be taken as from 18 to 60 years of age, then, in a population whose average death-rate would be, say, 40 per thousand, the normal death-rate of healthy males between these ages would not exceed 15 per thousand. That is to say, there should have been in France about 6,000,000 men available to answer this appeal. Actually it appears that on January 1, 1794, not more than 770,000 were present under arms, and there was one official at home for every two soldiers at the front. The estimates for 1793, which were, in fact, largely exceeded, make the average cost of these soldiers 1800 francs, an enormous figure for those days, principally accounted for by cost of new arms and equipment and leakage.

and order and henceforward submitted with reasonable willingness to necessary restraint.

The degree to which desertion in these levies attained can be estimated from the following letter addressed by La Coste to the Convention, dated Nancy, August 31, 1792:

> More than 140,000 armed citizens organised in battalions, with several companies of Cavalry, Grenadiers, guns and gunners are on the march to Weissenburg. . . .

But nothing was heard of their arrival until on the 10th September the Adjutant-General of the Army of the Rhine writes reporting the arrival of 1200 *agriculturists* with many weapons, but no soldiers. This was all that arrived out of the great column.[2] Such were the materials out of which the troops Mack encountered in the Netherlands had been formed and one can hardly wonder at the low estimate he put upon the fighting value of the French Army. Our own officers in the Duke of York's command fully shared it. But in the following years the goodwill of the few who withstood the temptation to desert, and the ruthless energy displayed by the Representatives of the People in enforcing discipline and order, together with the ceaseless practice in minor warfare which went on between the outposts, soon began to evolve a very different degree of efficiency. Already in 1794 the Austrians found them very much more difficult to beat, though their staying power in a campaign was of a very low order. They were still quite incapable of carrying through any operation involving more than a few days' march into the enemy's territory. Under the temptations of free quarters and plunder they simply disbanded themselves, and every advance came to an end by sheer want of numbers to go any farther.

The final fusion of the Regulars and Volunteers was the turning point of the whole evolution, and though carried

---

2. See Rousset: *Les Volontaires de 1791-4.*

out during the spring of the year, and in face of the enemy, the results soon showed themselves both in Germany and in Italy. Certainly in the former theatre of operations this newly acquired cohesion had almost given out before the Archduke Charles turned upon the French at Würzburg and Neresheim. But though the Austrians in this campaign proved ultimately victorious, the idea began to spread, particularly amongst the senior officers, that the French Army at last had become an actually superior fighting force taken unit by unit. In Italy, of course, those who had fought against Napoleon entertained no doubt on the subject at all, for essentially all Napoleon's victories during that campaign were due to the superior vigour and tenacity of the French soldiers, for whom no marches were too long, no numbers too formidable. But Mack had seen nothing of this transformation and naturally discounted the lugubrious stories he heard from the beaten generals.

As the period of extreme terror and tension relaxed, the defects in the drafting of this decree of 1793 became more and more evident, and the whole subject of Army Reform occupied again and again the attention of the succeeding Governments. Finally the whole was recast and submitted to the Council of Five Hundred by General Jourdan, and it was decreed (September 5, 1798) that every Frenchman was liable to military service from the twentieth to twenty-fifth year, and to the men thus liable the term *defenseurs consents* is applied for the first time.

How many of these men were to be called out and for how long depended on circumstances whether the country was at war or not. There was no fixed term of service qualifying for dismissal to the Reserves. Apparently there was no intention of forming any, and since for the next seventeen years the country was never at peace for more than three consecutive years, it would seem that the term of service was practically fixed by the man's ability to bear arms, and by nothing else. As the deaths during these years actually exceeded one million (though by how many it is impossible to state), it is evident that even a moderate rate of invaliding would have barely kept pace with the supply. It will be seen that this law permitted no exemption except from physical causes, and its operation pressed so intolerably upon the people in their shattered condition that, in the following year (1800), the provision of a paid substitute was sanctioned. This continued in force until 1870, when it proved one of the principal causes of the French downfall, as in practice it allowed the bulk of the middle classes to escape service, thus throwing the burden of defence on the upper and lower, "the froth and the dregs," to use an expression often applied to it by the opponents of the system.

In the space at my disposal it is utterly impossible to convey any adequate picture of the administrative work which fell upon the French War Office during this period in which Minister after Minister succeeded one another in rapid succession, and only Carnot, a Captain of Engineers, remained permanent.

I have alluded above to the creation of the "Demi-brigades" and the "Amalgam" in which Regulars and Volunteers were brigaded side by side, and ultimately fused altogether. Each of these steps entailed the disruption of hundreds of Volunteer units, and the absorption of thousands of officers, who, it is hardly necessary to add, resented their supersession or removal almost in proportion to their original unfitness for their posts. But the step gave the authorities the much needed power of selection, which they seem to have exercised with considerable discretion, judging from the uniform excellence of the commanders whom Napoleon took over when he became Emperor. Theirs was, indeed, a case of the "survival of the fittest" in a terribly hard school of selection, for not only had they been compelled to justify themselves by their acts in the face of the enemy, but to maintain control over their men, in spite of all risks of secret denunciation and political animosity.

Only born leaders of men could have survived such an ordeal. They may have been, indeed they often were, illiterate, rapacious, jealous and vindictive, *but they all possessed that power which defies all examinations to elicit viz. the power to get the last ounce of exertion and self-sacrifice out of the men under them, without recourse to legal formalities, or the application of authorised force.*

In a word, they were "crowd leaders," men who knew instinctively in each successive rank how to keep the dominant sentiment of the mass upon their side. When, for instance, at a later period Napoleon kept a whole Hussar brigade out under a heavy artillery fire as a punishment for unsteadiness in a previous action, he knew he was safe in doing so, because the majority of the Army strongly disapproved of cowardice under fire. But he would have been quite powerless to compel the same Hussars to groom their horses up to the Prussian standard, because the whole weight of opinion in the Service was against such a practice, and this tendency ran through every grade of the whole Army, and in itself constituted a moral factor sufficient to account almost entirely for its numerous successes.

In long-service Armies, trained in peace time, this "art of command" is generally absent, for nothing over occurs to compel a young officer to exert the spark of it which in varying degrees we all possess. In a wise system of training, things would be so arranged that such opportunities would have to be faced, but this is difficult, as they are always unpopular to all except the "elect," who rejoice in them. Still in our own case, with the facilities our Territorial system presents, it would be easy to arrange for such an interchange of officers from time to time amongst the several battalions, that all should find an opportunity of learning how to enforce obedience without recourse to authority, and in that way we might find a compensation for many defects in our organisation when it is compared with the machinelike exactitude of other nations.

It was out of these difficult circumstances by which the

French officers were surrounded that the system of decentralisation of command which led to the formation, first, of the "Division," ultimately to that of the "Army Corps" developed.

Since without ingrained respect for the "rank" mutual personal knowledge between men and officers was the only bond which could be relied upon, it became the custom to keep the General who had won the confidence of his men at the head of the same units as long as possible, and then to give him the freest possible hand in their command. It had, of course, long been the practice to place Generals at the heads of detachments of the three Arms, which were, in fact, Corps, but these detachments were only formed *ad hoc*, and generally melted away into the Army when they rejoined headquarters. There was no distinct bond of connection between the units and their Commander, and above all, no staff mechanism for the circulation of orders to units. During the early years of the Revolutionary Wars, when an Austrian General wished to order an operation, he had to write, or cause to be written by his clerks, separate orders in detail to each of the units in his command, a process in which so much time was lost that the orders almost invariably arrived too late.[3]

The French Corps Commander had merely to send an order to each of his three or four units, who then passed on the essential portion of each to the Brigades, and so forth, according to the system of the present day, and in this lay the chief secret of their superior mobility. There is nothing to show that a Prussian or Austrian battalion could not march as fast and as far along a highroad as a French one indeed, the presumption is that both in physique and in training the latter were inferior to the longer service men of other nations; but the fact remains that, whereas French Army Corps could

3. See two complaints, one by Beaulieu in 1796, the other by Mack in 1805, both clamouring for more clerks, in the Austrian Krugs Archive.

average twenty miles a day, and could be pushed to thirty-five, their enemies, owing to this vicious want of system in the circulation of orders, could rarely manage ten miles a day, and often fell as low as six and seven.

This was the essential secret of French mobility on which in turn Napoleon's strategy depended, and in no campaign is its advantage more apparent than in the one under consideration, for had the French averaged five miles a day less, the whole combination of Jena would have been impossible.

Lastly, we must call attention to an innovation in the conduct of War, due to Carnot's genius, which, though in advance of the means at his disposal, formed the stepping-stone for Napoleon's progress. We have seen that it had been the custom to form detachments of all arms for special missions in all countries, but it had never occurred to anyone to use these detachments in combination for a special offensive. When, for instance, Frederick the Great projected an offensive, he united his whole Army for the purpose, only leaving behind such detachments as were necessary for purely defensive purposes they might within their own sphere operate offensively for the attack was generally admitted as the soundest form of defence but their movement was never combined with the main Army on an ulterior objective.

Carnot initiated the idea of combining the operations of several Armies, two or more, in an advance on a single objective, such as Vienna in 1796, in which the Armies of Jourdan from the lower Rhine, of Moreau from the middle Rhine, and of Napoleon in Italy were all directed upon Vienna. As already stated, the idea was beyond the means of execution available wireless telegraphy alone would have justified the risk but it formed the point of departure for Napoleon's principle of combining his Army Corps upon the battlefield to which all his subsequent successes were due.

It is now time to turn to the specific development of the latter's methods and to trace step by step how these evolved themselves into a definite system, the essence of which was, that no matter what the enemy did, or did not do, Napoleon was certain to unite a numerical superiority against him.

In his *Education Militaire de Napoleon*, Captain Colin of the French General Staff has traced for us the gradual evolution of Napoleon's executive talent up to the Campaign of 1796, showing us the books he read and the type of mind with which he was brought into contact. Colonel Camon of the French Engineers has given us an admirable study of the spirit of the Emperor's Campaigns as derived from his own orders and correspondence; and we have in addition the admirable investigations of General Bonnal and General Foch, all from the standpoint of modern criticism, and based on the material found in the Archives of the French War Ministry.

These studies throw an entirely new light on the working of Napoleon's mind from day to day, and more especially enable us to discount the "evidential" value of his own Memoirs written at St Helena, also those of his Marshals and other contemporaries.

We no longer see him making plans of campaign complete to the smallest detail, far in advance of events; we are now able to follow him from day to day, with a great objective undeniably before him, but working for it by fresh resolutions conceived from hour to hour, as the reports of the enemy's movements come to hand; and meeting each emergency as it arises with an intuitive perception which at times seems little short of miraculous.

In his first Italian campaigns we find him still practising the precepts of his masters, which were indeed time-honoured and accepted by all his contemporaries in theory; but whereas they were tied and bound by practical considerations of supply and responsibility, he was relatively free from these restrictions. Hence he was able to apply them with a vigour and boldness to which the eighteenth century could afford no parallel. Concentration on the decisive point was no novelty; every other general of the period would gladly have anticipated his example had they been able to do so, but because of the utter want of system for circulating information and orders which prevailed in their armies, Napoleon's concentrations were always finished before their own.

Nor was there a general in Europe who was not equally well aware of the advantage to be gained by threatening an enemy's communications; most of them knew only too well from bitter experience how fatally demoralising to the troops was the mere rumour of danger to their lines of supply and retreat. But they knew, as practical men, that the threat at their enemy's communication involved the exposure of their own, and that as opposed to Napoleon they had the most to lose.

For the French had been forced by circumstances to learn to do without luxuries, and dragged no interminable train behind them. If the enemy captured their bivouac grounds, they were no better off than before, for the Republican troops left no supplies behind them, whereas if their enemy succeeded in manoeuvring them out of their positions, it was in practice impossible to prevent their finding food, arms, equipment and ammunition. If they failed in their undertakings, they had an outraged King and Cabinet to face and an established position to lose. If Napoleon failed he risked only his head, and heads sat lightly on French shoulders during those first terrible years.

The conditions, therefore, were quite unequal, and it needed only audacity and the driving energy of an almost superhuman character to carry the French Army to victory. It was this need that Napoleon abundantly supplied, but it was a very risky game to play; and when at Marengo his concentration failed, *for the reason that he had allowed his enemy time to concentrate first,* he set his mind to work to find some safer basis for his projects, and found it for the moment *in the training of his Cavalry to form the "Cavalry Screen."*

It was in reliance on this system that he entered upon

the Campaign of Ulm in 1805. Covered by a Cavalry screen a couple of days' march in front of his Infantry columns, he adapted his manoeuvres to the movements of his enemy quite in the manner of the modern German school, whose practice in 1870 shows no advance upon his original conception. But Napoleon soon found out *that though Cavalry could observe, it possessed in itself no power to hold*; and it was quickly evident to him *that the presence of an enemy at a given spot on a given date was no sure indication of where that enemy might happen to be forty-eight hours later.*

The problem is, in fact, insoluble a priori, for only the other side can be aware of all the factors which enter into the decision, and even then no two minds are likely to appreciate these several factors at the same valuation.

With regard to the tactics of the Army Napoleon employed to gain his strategic ends they may best be visualised as the survival of the fittest under the new conditions which had been evolved from the social chaos of the French Revolution. This does not imply that they were ideal solutions in themselves, better than any that had gone before them (which in fact they certainly were not), but that they represented the best use to which the available raw material could be applied for the attainment of the purpose in view. This is only another way of stating Moltke's definition of the Art of War.[4]

The French had entered upon the great Revolutionary Wars with drill-books copied exactly from the original Prussian model. But their raw levies were quite incapable of the accurate manoeuvring under fire which had distinguished the long-service soldiers of Frederick the Great, the topographical conditions differed widely, and the fundamental condition which alone made possible the long advances of twenty and thirty battalions in line (*viz.* acquired cavalry superiority on the Prussian side), was entirely wanting.

---

4. Moltke's definition runs as follows: "The art of war consists in making the best practical use of the means at hand for the attainment of the object in view."

A single deployed line of these raw soldiers could not endure the inevitable losses which the attempt to close in to decisive range without firing invariably entailed. Hence arrangements had to be made for a succession of lines, each intended to carry the one in front forward when once it had halted to fire the same idea is current in all Armies nowadays. But if the first line failed to stand and broke back upon its followers, the result was generally a rapid retreat of the whole; mass. Hence, to guard against this danger, gaps had to be left in the following lines which could be rapidly closed by deployment, when the necessity arose, and a line of small columns (weak battalions of perhaps 400 men) soon established itself as the most practical solution.

Seen from the enemy's side, such an attack gave an exact replica of the normal advances practised throughout Europe after 1870 and incidentally explains their origin. The enemy—say the Prussians—seeing a ragged, badly dressed crowd of men approaching them, with further little clumps following behind, never supposed for a moment that these were in any way an imitation of their own "proud and beautiful line." They assumed that the French had discovered a new secret of victory the advance of the individual fighter as distinguished from the true skirmisher, whose use they fully understood. Hence, when disaster ultimately overtook their own more perfect formations, the whole Army conceived the conviction that in some way or other the crowded ragged firing line, with the little company columns following on behind it, contained in itself the spirit of the French Infantry. This picture remained in their minds through all the years of reform that followed after Jena, and first found full literary expression in the works of May, Boguslowski, Tellenbach and countless other less remembered names.

As pointed out in the previous chapter, the skill of the Austrian Light Infantry over broken ground had from the very first compelled the French to evolve a similar type, the Voltigeurs, to encounter them.

These troops, profiting also by the experience gained in American and Canadian warfare, very soon equalled, if they did not surpass, their original model. Hence they soon became the idols of the Army, and instinctively the Line battalions sought to emulate their example, with the consequence that the regular Infantry soon threw off the excessive pedantry of the original Prussian model, and the whole Infantry, even before Napoleon came to handle it, had became an exceedingly supple and powerful weapon ready to his hands. It was equally capable of holding its own in forest or mountain, and of changing its formations rapidly and accurately to meet the ever-varying conditions of long-protracted battles. On the other hand, while careful at all times to be ready to meet a charge of Cavalry or a temporary reverse to the other troops around them, they had as firm a faith in the volleys and file fire of the deployed line (*en bataille*, as they called it) as was possessed by either the British or the Prussians before them.

But in all these years the French Army had never reached the point at which it could be fought in battle as a whole; that was to come afterwards when the gradual deterioration of the Infantry, the improvement in the mobility of the Field Artillery forced a complete readjustment upon the Emperor. At Castiglione Napoleon had indeed handled a corps as a unit and made full use of the powers of a small Artillery reserve, but in general the combats against the Allies and Austrians had been combats of detachments. Division fought against Division, in which the sum of the results, good or bad, decided the ultimate retreat of one side or the other, and when the day was over there was no available mass of reserves on either side to give the final decision and initiate a true pursuit.

Neither the great Artillery Commander or the Cavalry Leader had as yet appeared, and though in his pursuit of Werneck Murat showed the promise of his future achievement after Jena, the campaign of Ulm was singularly destitute of lessons of tactical importance.

To sum up the whole chapter, let us picture to ourselves a Light Infantry as tenacious and conscious of mastery in their own special branch as the Rifles and Jagers of modern armies, a Line Infantry trained on much the same lines, but still adhering to the slower and more deliberate methods of the old "decision-compelling" advance; a Cavalry capable of daring and brilliant actions by squadrons, but far too little trained in equitation to be susceptible of employment in great masses; and an Artillery mobile and alert to seize chances by batteries, but, like the Cavalry, still without the uniformity of training which can alone render it possible to transfer "masses" of 100 guns and upwards rapidly and certainly from point to point of the battlefield. These movements are not essentially conditioned by the weapons in use (for death remains the same, however inflicted, and a man's life was worth fewer hours of purchase then than it is nowadays) but depend finally, with all mounted Arms, on the thoroughness with which the troops have been trained beforehand, and the character of the Man who commands them. How Senarmont would have smiled at the butcher's bills in his own Arm of the Service of the present day.

Chapter 3

Political Factors Influencing Austrian Operations

The simplest way in which an English student can obtain a firm grasp of the principles underlying military action on the continent of Europe at the close of the eighteenth century is to picture to himself the Kings and Princes then in power as so many English county families, possessing the same "earth hunger," but instead of the old-established firms of solicitors, the recognised instruments by which our landowners sought to extend or round off their estates, the various Royalties employed equally carefully selected diplomatists and politicians, with an ultimate appeal to armed force, whereas in England the law of the land compelled the final decision. In all these intrigues, having the extension of their estates as an object, the wishes of the inhabitants were as little considered as they are nowadays in this country when a great property changes hands. War on one frontier hardly interrupted for a moment the course of absorption on another, and generally the object of further acquisitions, either by marriage, barter or force, was kept steadily in view from generation to generation.

At the outbreak of the French revolutionary wars this process was in full operation over the whole extent of South Germany, and Austria and Prussia had already acquired, by one means or another, large outlying properties which interfered very materially with the political frontiers of the South German estates, and modified most essentially the conduct of military operations.

The Prussian possession of Ansbach hampered a French offensive from the north, and in the south it will be noticed that an almost continuous belt of Austrian outlying territory extends from the Inn to the banks of the Rhine about Freiburg and Breisach.

The possession of these districts, and the neutrality of Ansbach were vitally important to the Austrian Empire, and dictated time after time the main lines of any operations against France, because in all these districts in which Austria possessed particular interest her troops could move as in the home countries, and magazines could be accumulated and contracts issued with a freedom impossible in the territories of other reigning princes.

The fortress of Ulm thus became of paramount importance under all circumstances, for if Bavaria threw in her interests with the empire it closed all the great avenues of approach, as long as the neutrality of Ansbach was respected; while if Bavaria remained neutral, or joined the French, a force based upon Ulm possessed in their extremest form all the advantages usually accorded to a re-entrant line of frontier. Napoleon at Milan in 1800 held a position intrinsically far less secure than did Mack at Ulm in 1805, for whereas the former could not count either on his communications over the St Gothard Pass or his magazines about Zurich, for one hour longer than his flag was in the ascendant, Mack could, and no doubt would, had he been an independent Monarch, have accumulated stores and reserves all along the northern shores of Lake Constance and drawn reinforcements over the Alps to his assistance through relatively friendly territories. Unfortunately for Austria, Mack was not a reigning Sovereign, and the attention of her statesmen was concentrated on dangers other than those which actually arose.

How this happened must always remain a mystery, for Napoleon had, in fact, in 1803, given the Austrian Court ample warning[1] of the direction of attack which he intended to select. It was in October 1803 that Russia first approached Austria with a view to the formation of a fresh coalition, and in December of the same year offered to mobilise within eight days a force of 170,000 men, half to operate either with or against the Prussians, half with the Austrians, and these proposals were at once submitted to the Archduke Charles for consideration and report.

The Archduke was intensely set against war, for no one knew better than he the shortcomings of the Army, the poverty of the Treasury or the unreliability of Russian promises. It was on the 3rd March 1804 that he submitted a memoir on the whole subject from which the following extracts are taken:

> Our financial situation is 'detestable'. It is impossible to re-establish the equilibrium between expenditure and receipts even in peace. At least 80 million florins are necessary to place the army on a war footing, 33 millions a year to keep it up, and 150 millions at least for each year's active operations. This would spell bankruptcy at very short notice, for so much paper money has already been issued, and our credit is so low that it is impossible to get further loans taken up. No doubt there will be subsidies from England, but we must not exaggerate their importance. They only diminish, they do not annul the expenses of the war. In fact, the amount indicated, 37 millions florins, is a mere fraction of the total expense, and Great Britain will take care to recoup herself first for sums still due on previous advances.
>
> Our resources in men are almost equally inadequate. We have only 25 millions of population to oppose to

1 See *Napoleon to Luchesini*, 27th Nov. 1803.

the 40 millions under French dominion *viz.* 25 millions in France, the balance in her new acquisitions, and the conscription so far has hardly touched the people in these latter at all. In the Hereditary States of the Empire, cases of exemption are very numerous, and previous levies have already made serious inroads on the remainder. Altogether we should need 108,598 men to bring the army to war establishments, and the last census only traced out 83,159. Hence it is not even possible to complete the Army, still less to recruit it to supply the waste of active operations, and finally if we take up these 83,000 men, it will give the death-blow to our agriculture and commerce, which are already in very evil case.[2]

Hence hostilities should be avoided at all costs. We can only contemplate it as a possibility if we have Allies, and who will these Allies be? There are only the Russians who have uniformly urged Austria on to fight and never moved at all until in 1798, they knew Bonaparte was safely locked up in Egypt and who can trust them? Who can tell on what trumpery pretext, differences of opinion between commanders, etc., the promised support may not be withdrawn. Finally, in any case, Austria will have to bear the first shock of the campaign, and perhaps the invaders will be in possession of her Capital before the Russians can arrive.

It is said that war is inevitable, perhaps so, but we can at least avoid anything to hasten it, and every year will improve our relative position.

The French Official Account, whose abbreviated version of the original I am here following, adds in a note that in another report the Archduke advises that Austria should under

2. Before the war was over, many times 83,000 men had been found, and commerce and agriculture still continued.

no circumstances interfere with Napoleon's projected invasion of England, in the success of which he did not believe, but which in any case must cripple French offensive power for many years to come. This conviction must be borne in mind in estimating the value of the whole of the previous report, and its marked pessimistic tendency. He continues:

> If by misfortune the war nevertheless does break out, let us see what will be the consequences, and this brings us to examine the plan of operations to be pursued.
>
> The front upon which the struggle will be waged *extends from the Austro-Italian frontiers to Lake Constance*; it is from thence that we shall advance if we take the offensive, or stand to fight if we decide to await the attack. *It seems quite indisputable that the bulk of our forces should be allotted to the Italian theatre of operations.* On our side, because it is only in that direction that we can look for an acquisition (of territory understood) of any sufficient value, and because it is from that side that the danger to the monarchy is both greatest and nearest; finally because it is only by taking the offensive or by maintaining our position in Italy that we can save the Hereditary States from invasion.
>
> On the part of the French, because their Government has the greatest interest in preserving the Italian Republic; because also it is from them that the French Armies can by their first movements most injure our Empire, attaining by a single victory across an unfortified frontier, the very heart and capital of the nation; finally because in such an advance, the enemy would have its resources immediately behind its front on the borders of Italy and Switzerland, and will be nearer to its points of support and reinforcements; whereas, by marching on Vienna by Suabia and Bavaria, their armies would have much further to go before striking a decisive blow.

> This consideration is of importance because of the desirability of achieving a result before the Russians can intervene. *Hence it is on the Adige that we must expect the first and principal operations, and it is there that the Austrian Armies should assume the offensive.*

Then follows a long catalogue of topographical difficulties discussed with all the verbosity current at that period, which we can afford to disregard, and the memoir then continues:

> To support the operations of the Austrian Army of Italy, and to keep the enemy out of Tyrol, it will be necessary to oppose a second army, much less numerous, to the force which the French will probably send from Strassburg, by the shortest line to Vienna through Suabia. *This should strive to anticipate the enemy upon the Iller.* However one or several victories gained on this side would have no other result than to drive the enemy back upon the Rhine, where he possesses lines of fortresses within which it would be disastrous to attempt to follow him . . . *such an idea could not enter the head of any reasonable tactician.*
>
> Hence nothing can be done in Germany until the Army of Italy has crossed the Adda as the consequence of a victorious engagement one can only choose a good defensive position which will cover the Tyrol against the enemy's incursions, and prevent a French Army from entering Austria down the valley of the Danube.

I have given this singular document at some length, as to my mind it serves to clear up the fundamental mystery why Mack so suddenly sprang again into favour over the head of the Archduke Charles, the victor of 1796. What possible use could any Government, knowing itself to be compelled to fight, find for such a persistent pessimist, and what would any reasonable statesman or diplomatist make of such an incoherent, loosely reasoned, badly supported piece of work, the outcome apparently of some six months' study?

It will be noted that the Archduke begins by fixing the limits of the theatre of operations as between the Austro-Italian frontier and Lake Constance, and then never refers to this district again. Probably this was only done to note his general adherence to the line of action long before thought out by the Austrian headquarters in 1796, 1798 and 1799, and with which Clausewitz dealt so scathingly throughout his works. Clausewitz imagined that the Austrian School of War pinned its faith on the possession of commanding ground owing to some fancied analogy between the action of water running down hill and the flood of invasion sweeping down on the plains similarly accelerated by the force of gravity. This, however, is one of the cases in which Clausewitz's judgment became obscured by the contempt with which Austrian dilatoriness during the latter campaigns of the Great War had filled him. In fact the Austrians, as C. von B. K. has shown at length, had very substantial grounds indeed for their attitude on this subject, and it is a pity for them that they did not adhere to this portion of their doctrine consistently, and prepare the country within their own frontier to give effect to it. Actually the possession of Switzerland was of transcendent importance to the Austrians, on the assumption, which they had every reasonable right to make, that their battalions and Light Infantry were still, unit for unit, superior to the French levies.

The exit from the mountain passes into the Italian plains could always be forced in those days by disciplined troops prepared to stand up to heavy punishment without risk of panic; and the north of Switzerland gave them not only good through roads from Chur and along the left bank of Lake Constance and down the Rhine to Schaffhausen, but it afforded them also the advantage of water communication from Bregenz, through the Lake and down the river to the same place. Thirty miles of this at least could not be interfered with, and the remaining fifty could easily be guarded by a few squadrons of horse hovering to the northward in the plains about Donaueschingen.

Austrian troops had again and again marched over the same districts, and armies had crossed the Rhine repeatedly between Constance and Schaffhausen, and these districts still remained, as in 1798 and 1799, the shortest and most direct way to the heart of the French territory. As for means of communication on the water, and roads over the mountains into the Valley of the Inn, abundant resources lay to their hands had they thought about utilising them during the year's respite that still lay before them. Whether anything to improve these communications through the Voralgebirge was actually accomplished I have been unable to ascertain, and would only note in passing that, judging from Indian frontier road-making experience, no serious obstacles to such improvements existed at any point. Meanwhile the impression remains strong in my mind, from several incidents in Mack's subsequent movements, that he had fully grasped the intrinsic value of Switzerland as a base, and did in fact strive to have the roads improved, and more boats put on the lake. He would have taken full advantage of all the facilities Switzerland afforded had he not been fatally misled as to the strength of the troops arrayed against him, and thereby led to persist in offensive operations long after all reasonable chances for success had disappeared.

Be this as it may, the fact remains that this lugubrious prophecy of the Archduke's did not prevent the signature of a contract of alliance between Austria and Russia on the 4th November 1804, and the military Cabinets immediately proceeded to draw up a plan of combined operations.

This was transmitted to St Petersburg on the 13th March 1805, and seems to have been the work of a "paste and scissors" committee. Most of the long-winded, loosely reasoned passages of the archduke are reproduced, while other paragraphs calculated to relieve their despondency are intercalated, which seem to breathe the spirit of Mack, and the only material departure from the original lies in the selection of the line of the "Lech" for the deployment of the army of Southern Germany, a line which was certainly not the selection either of Mack or the Archduke, and indicates that whoever was responsible for its insertion had not grasped the spirit of the original doctrine of the importance of Switzerland, although this point is treated at considerable length in the document.

This plan was submitted to the Emperor of Russia by General Stutterheim with another long memoir of his own dated 6th April, to which the Russian General Staff responded, promising 90,000 men to act in Germany (and 25,000 for the kingdom of Naples) to be divided into two—Armies Army Corps we should call them nowadays. These were both to operate on the left bank of the Danube. The memoir also approved, in general, of the Austrian proposals, only protesting against the very pessimistic attitude assumed by the Court of Vienna as to its resources compared with those of France. It pointed out, what was undoubtedly true, that Bonaparte himself was in equally desperate straits for want of ready money, and that his resources in men were not nearly as great as the Austrians imagined them to be.

Whilst these negotiations were in progress, the Russians signed a treaty of alliance with Great Britain (11th April) in which the contingents to be furnished by Austria, and the amount of subsidies she was to receive, were regulated precisely as if that Power had been a consenting party to the deed. The news of this high-handed action caused lively emotion at Vienna, but so great appeared the risks that two months were allowed to elapse before a reply was sent to St Petersburg. The Russians now, by a note dated 29th June, called on Austria to state definitely whether she would adhere to her declarations of the 4th November. They further announced that not only had the orders to mobilise 180,000 men in Russia been issued, but that they counted on obtaining another 100,000 from Prussia, Saxony and Denmark, and that Sweden had already consented to find 16,000. Austria on her side must now mobilise 250,000—*i.e.* the number stipulated in the abovementioned declaration of the 4th November.

The Archduke and his party nevertheless continued to urge upon the Emperor the policy of peace at any price, insisting as before on the unreliability of Russian promises, and the certainty that Austria would have to stand up to the first blows of the French unsupported; while, either to strengthen his hands, or from sheer conviction on his own part, General Duka, the Q.M.G. of the Army, showed that there were only 39,635 men with 3,398 horses present with the Colours, and that when all the men on furlough had been recalled the Army would still be 41,767 men short even of its peace establishment. For this despondent view of the situation, he was promptly removed to the command of the district of Temesvar, about the furthest point from the threatened frontier that could be found. (Angeli, *Ulm and Austerlitz*). Cobenzl, who had succeeded Thugut, now brought forward Mack, on whose optimism he could rely, to encourage the Emperor to adhere to the Russian proposals, and Mack, who had imbibed the true essence of the French national spirit, was not slow in availing himself of his opportunity.

For this he is roundly blamed by the authors of the French *Official History* of the campaign[3], whose account I am here following, but in doing this I submit they are judging after the event. Surely Mack as a soldier, and personally of exceptional courage, can hardly be condemned for believing, after his years of experience against the French revolutionary armies, that *the strength of a nation depends far more on the will to fight in the individual soldier* than on the precision in drill and perfection of turnout in the organised units which together

3. Which account was based on the Austrian documents and canards promulgated by Mack's enemies.

go to make up the Army? He believed, and not without reason, that the secret of French successes lay *primarily in mobility, next in the personality of the leader*, and finally *in the cause for which the Nation was fighting*. Moreover, there was nothing in the facts, as far as they were known to him at the time, to lead him to believe that in any one of these qualifications he himself and his countrymen were inferior to their opponents. Napoleon, it is true, had beaten his old superior officers out of Italy twice over, but he knew these men well and their limitations, and in view of his own rapid and unparalleled rise in the most aristocratic and caste ridden service in the world, and the astounding influence which his presence in the field had again and again exerted over the troops, who can blame him if he felt fairly competent to cross swords with the leader whose reputation came to him only through highly coloured accounts? In brief, he trusted his men, and he trusted himself; he only failed to realise the disloyalty of his immediate instruments *viz*. the band of courtiers who surrounded his Chief. It is necessary to insist on this point of view at the outset, for if the study of the campaign is undertaken under the influence of the glamour which has since accumulated around the Napoleonic legend, no useful lesson can possibly be derived from its study. The French authors continue:

> We should deceive ourselves greatly if we imagine that Mack was an object of admiration to the whole Austrian Army his false science deceived no one except the politicians.

But who in the Austrian army of that day was qualified to decide whether Mack's "science" was false or not? Were not his Austrian critics the very men who accused Napoleon of having defeated them because he did not even realise the accepted rules of civilised war? There were many first-rate fighting men still in the French Army, and for many years afterwards, who agreed essentially with these Austrian commanders in this. But the merit which the Austrian statesmen saw in Mack was precisely this that he never made difficulties, and that he recognised that in war *the object is to beat the enemy, not merely to avoid being beaten.*

That this view is at least defensible is evident from the first steps Mack took on his appointment *viz.* to decree that the army should live, like the French, on the country, and that the Transport Services should at once hand over all their best horses to the Artillery; this at least showed that he had grasped one of the chief factors of French successes mobility.

On the 7th July the courier bearing the definite adherence of Austria to the new coalition left Vienna, and on the 16th July, Mack, Schwartzenberg and Winzingerode met to arrange details of cooperation. It was agreed that the Russians should form three Armies. The first, commanded by Kutusow and comprising 54,918 men, 7900 horses and 200 guns, was timed to reach Braunau on the Inn on the 16th October. The troops were to have one day's rest in four, and no daily march was to exceed twenty miles. This is important in view of the delays which ultimately took place which could not have been foreseen by Mack. Kutusow was to be subordinate to the Emperor and the Archduke Charles, but was not to receive orders from any other Austrian generals.

The second Army under Benningsen (39 battalions, 85 squadrons, and 24 guns) was to follow closely on the heels of the first, unless called on to support the third. This Army, under Buxhoewden, 33 battalions, and 35 squadrons (no artillery mentioned), was to move by Bohemia into Franconia, keeping an eye upon Prussia, whose attitude was still equivocal. On this basis a definite treaty between Russia and Austria was signed on the 9th August 1805, and this notwithstanding the vehement protests of the Archduke Charles, who pointed out the many difficulties in the way of provisioning the Russians—the want of peas, haricots, lentils, etc., which were not grown in the districts traversed. Yet armies have lived without these necessaries in other climates, and the Russian *moujik* was never a particularly delicate feeder.

Already in the month of May, Mack had been at work, with as much secrecy as possible, preparing the Army for hostilities. In addition to the transfer of horses from the Train to the Artillery, already referred to, men had been called to the colours on various pretexts, horses had been bought, provisions stored, and camps had been formed at Pettau and in Illyria. Unfortunately he had not stopped at this, but had endeavoured to introduce many reforms in organisation, which, though sound in principle, upset existing regulations just when continuity of practice was most necessary.

With regard to the principal change *viz.* acceptance of the methods of requisition in place of the former plan of supply by magazines it is difficult to see how mobility and artillery power could have been provided by any other method. Both of these measures were essential to his designs, but in practice the attempt failed from causes which Mack and his contemporaries were not psychologists enough to foresee. You cannot by the stroke of a pen alter the deep-rooted sentiments of a long-service Army, indeed of any Army at all. It was all very well to order the troops to live on the country—*i.e.* to turn themselves into hordes of licensed freebooters—but the whole tradition of this wholesale foraging had died out since the time of the Thirty Years' War, and neither men nor officers knew how to adapt themselves to their new roles. They might have done better in an enemy's country; our own troops in Afghanistan learnt such procedure quite readily from the Sikhs and Ghurkhas. But Mack's misfortune was, that the South German people, speaking the same language, were not enemies at all. The troops would persist in regarding them as irresponsible victims of very cruel circumstances, and it was this attitude of mind which primarily contributed to Napoleon's successes by rendering it possible for his soldiers (who were thoroughly at home in this phase of the struggle for the survival of the fittest) to find food enough to exist upon in the very same districts in which the Austrians had already nearly starved. This fact requires to be underlined, and to be particularly remembered.[4]

Mack's zeal and activity in pushing on all these changes, and his obstinate determination to overcome all difficulties, contrasted so markedly with the pessimism of the Archduke Charles and his particular clique that he completely conquered the Emperor's confidence, and for the time became the virtual dictator of the whole military situation. Thus on the 15th August he submitted a note to the Emperor demanding—1st, that the Archduke Charles should at once take up the command of the Army in Italy; 2nd, that the Emperor himself should forthwith assume the command-in-chief, appointing Mack as his Q.M.G. with power to correspond directly with the other Q.M.G.'s; 3rd, that the Corps in the district around Trent should be placed under the orders of the Archduke John, who commanded in the Tyrol; 4th, that Bavaria should be invaded in the early days of September in order to facilitate the absorption of the Bavarian army—to all of which the Imperial sanction was at once forthcoming.

With the Archduke Charles in Italy, the assumption of the chief command by the Emperor became a necessity, since, according to the protocol with the Russians, their commanders could only take orders from the Monarch himself. Pending the Russian arrival, there was practically no command for the Emperor to assume, and hence no duties for his Q.M.G., it was therefore decided to give the command of the wing of the army destined to act in Germany to the young Archduke Ferdinand, and to send Mack with him nominally as his Chief of the Staff, trusting that the young Prince would loyally carry out Mack's intentions, which indeed he was strictly enjoined

4. Almost identically the same thing happened to the Germans in 1870 when their armies were ordered to live on the country. See *Studien zur Kriegsgeschichte und Taktik*, Vol. ÜI., Generalstab, Berlin.

to do by the Emperor himself. Unfortunately, the Prince developed too much character and too little intelligence, as the sequel will presently show.[5]

The incompatibility of disposition between these two men, the Archduke Ferdinand and Mack, destined so unfortunately to run in double harness, was not long in disclosing itself. At a council of war held at Hetzendorf, 20th August, at which the plan of campaign drawn up by the Archduke Charles was read and discussed, the Prince observed that Napoleon would be at Munich with 150,000 men before the Russians could arrive on the Inn, and he advised, in consequence, that only a corps of observation, some 30,000 to 40,000 strong, should be sent into Bavaria, with orders merely to reconnoitre and requisition, retreating, if necessary, before the enemy's advance. In this advice the Archduke Charles and Feldzeugmeister Zach concurred, even the Emperor momentarily assenting also. But Mack had no difficulty with his flow of persuasive eloquence in establishing that Napoleon could not pass the Rhine with more than 70,000 men, as he had certainly 20,000 in his hospitals, and must leave 30,000 to 40,000 more on the coast demonstrating against the British, while 20,000 must keep order in Paris, and Mack being supported by Cobenzl, the Emperor finally came round to this opinion.

One would like to have further details of the discussion in order to decide whether the young Prince's figures, which so closely accorded with the subsequent event, were the result of a lucky guess only, or of reasoned conviction. Looking at the facts as far as they were known at the time, the presumption is in favour of the guess guided by the pessimism

5. Though the Prince was only in his twenty-fifth year, he had already seen much service. In 1799 he had distinguished himself at Pfullendorf and Stokach and in 1800 he had commanded a Light Brigade under Kray, and had done good service, notably at Biberach, for which he received the Maria Theresa Order and had been made General of Cavalry in 1805. The rank of Field Marshal had also been conferred on him, to give him the necessary superiority of rank for his present command.

prevailing amongst the Archduke Charles' surroundings. The young Prince saw in his imagination the whole of Napoleon's Army singling out his command for its undivided attentions, and did not see how completely this assumption struck at the root of the whole plan of campaign before him, whilst he could not be aware of Napoleon's intended violation of the neutrality of Ansbach, on which, ultimately, Napoleon's arrival at Munich about the specified date actually depended. Finally, the mere idea of moving even 150,000 men from the shores of the English Channel to Munich, within the time limit that the Prince's prognostication carried with it, would, under any other circumstances, have been laughed out of court at once by any assemblage of Staff College graduates of any other country but France at that period, for nothing of the kind had ever been attempted or thought of until Napoleon actually accomplished it. Had it been otherwise, the feat itself would hardly have caused such universal amazement. We can readily picture Mack, the past master in the logistics of his period, crumbling into pieces the pessimistic predictions of his youthful Commander, and also how the after consequences, when the happy guess of the younger man was so singularly confirmed by the event, would be all the greater in proportion to the thoroughness and efficiency with which the teacher had performed his task. Ultimately, however, the Archduke Charles' plan was definitely adopted, subject to slight alterations due to the actual situation of the units of the whole Army.

There were at this moment 171 battalions and 95 squadrons (94,600 men) in Italy, and in the district around Trent, 28 battalions and 6 squadrons (12,100 men)—in all, 106,700 men. The Archduke John had 22,000 men in the Tyrol, and the "Army of Germany," as Prince Ferdinand's command was designated, comprised 88 battalions and 48 squadrons, say 60,000 men; whilst 35 battalions and 18 squadrons remained behind in the interior of the Monarchy.

Active operations were to commence in Italy by the capture of Mantua and Peschiera as preliminaries to acquiring the country round Milan. There would then be a temporary halt until the Army of Germany, united with the Russians, had established themselves firmly in Suabia.

The Army of Germany was to penetrate into Bavaria, following the roads along the foot-hills of the Alps, so as to gain ground as quickly as possible, carrying the war into the enemy's country, capturing his Army and securing the outlets from the Tyrol.

> If the French, operating on the left bank of the Danube, threatened Ulm or Regensburg, a position was to be taken up about Munich facing towards the river, or *the river itself was to be crossed higher up to threaten the enemy's communications*, until the arrival of reinforcements rendered it possible to fight a decisive battle.

The plan then goes on to specify what should be done after all the fortresses had been captured, and all the battles won, and is perhaps one of the best examples of selling the bear's skin before the animal has been caught which history has preserved.

The words in italics indicate without doubt Mack's contribution, the rest is the undiluted wisdom of the Eighteenth-Century school, to which the Archduke had again reverted after his momentary emancipation in 1796.

On the 2nd September Mack took over the command of the troops already assembled at the Camp of Wels, pending the arrival of the young Archduke, and immediately he despatched the available force in two columns towards the Inn, which they were to cross on the 8th, their ultimate destination being Parsdorf and Freising respectively, which they were to reach on the 13th September. The northern column under Klenau consisted of 15 battalions, 16 squadrons; the southern one under Gottesheim of 15 battalions, 15 squadrons; in both cases, the guns accompanying the troops forming part of the regimental establishments are not given. At the same time Jellacic's command in the Tyrol moved up in support of an advance guard under Wolfskeel from Bregenz to Ravensburg and Waldsee, thence to Biberach and the upper Danube, whilst the main body concentrated about Feldkirch on the Rhine above Lake Constance.

Behind this first echelon, there followed on the northern road, *via* Braunau, Riesch's Column of 12 battalions, 16 squadrons, and 1 heavy battery due at Braunau 17th September; and on the southern road Kienmayer's command of 13 battalions, 16 squadrons, 1 battery, due at Scharding on the Inn, 13th September; and behind both was Gyulai at Salzburg with 8 battalions, 16 squadrons, 1 battery in all 60 battalions, 78 squadrons in Bavaria, with 21 battalions, 6 squadrons in the Tyrol under Jellacic, with a total strength of 51,000 men. These were to be followed immediately by 39 battalions and 52 squadrons moving up to the frontier from the interior (another 30,000) giving in round figures 80,000 for the whole command.

The orders by which Mack set this Army in motion have not been published; fortunately, however, their issue threw the Archduke Charles into such a fury that he addressed a special report to the Emperor calling attention to the innumerable instances in which Mack had exceeded both his powers and the customs of the Austrian Army. From this report we get some insight into the absolute fearlessness with which Mack accepted all responsibility, and the determination he showed in getting things done. The Archduke's biographer would have been wiser had he suppressed this letter.

Meanwhile, on the 3rd September, Austria broke off diplomatic negotiations with France, and Prince Schwartzenberg was sent to the Elector of Bavaria at Munich to announce the coming War, and to solicit the Elector's support. He reached the Bavarian Court on the 6th, and the Elector assured him verbally of his intention to stand by the Austrians, referring him to the Minister for Foreign Affairs, Montgelas, for further details. Conferences accordingly took place on the two succeeding days, but on the night of the 8th the Elector himself slipped away towards Würzburg, and the Bavarian Army followed him, part towards Würzburg, part towards Bamberg. Finding that he had been deceived, Schwartzenberg rode back to Mack on the 9th inst., and the latter at once sent off flying columns, both to pursue the Bavarians and to cut off and seize supplies and stores, and break up all centres of mobilisation. These flying columns, of all arms, formed an advance screen of observation. The main bodies were also ordered to increase their marches and were timed now to reach the Iller, between Memmingen and Ulm, on the 19th September.

Mack himself reached the Iller on the 15th, and immediately commenced laying out works for the defence of the whole river line, concentrating particularly on Memmingen and Ulm, both needing but little to place them in security against a surprise attack. His activity was ceaseless, and we find him also at work about Ravensburg and Lindau, evidently seeing personally to his supply arrangements and communications with the Tyrol.

On the 19th September the Archduke Ferdinand assumed command of the army and signalised the event by ordering Kienmayer, Gyulai, and Riesch to halt, and the Advance Guard to keep behind the Iller. At the same time he wrote to Mack to rejoin at headquarters. Mack seems to have ignored this invitation, going on to Kempten, part of his tour of inspection, but he wrote to the Prince, adjuring him not to interfere with the orders already issued, and also to the Emperor, who had reached the front. This letter is so characteristic of Mack's attitude that it is reproduced practically in full:

19th Sept. 1805
To H. M. the Emperor
All except perhaps 10,000 to 12,000 men who remain

> to guard the coasts and southern frontier of France are moving on the Rhine, and soon two great French Armies will cross that river; one probably between Hüningen and Strassburg, the other between Mannhein and Mayence: the former against your Majesty's army on the Iller, the latter by Würzburg against the Russians coming from Bohemia. I entreat your Majesty most earnestly to approve the measures indicated in the project which accompanies this note, etc., etc.

To this appeal the Emperor proved amenable, and the troops were allowed to proceed to the destinations to which Mack had assigned them.

On the 21st September the Emperor and the Archduke went to Landsberg where they met Mack, and during the following two days the situation was fully discussed, especially the question of the possible violation of Ansbach, a question primarily for the Foreign Office and the Emperor, not for Mack in command of a Field Force. In his "Justification," subsequently published, Mack claims that neither the Emperor nor his advisers considered it within the limits of probability, *in view of the declarations they had received from the Prussian Court.*

Mack's mind being thus at rest as to the direction from which alone serious danger might threaten him, the following arrangements were agreed to on the 23rd September:

A Flank Guard consisting of Kienmayer's Corps of 16 battalions, 24 squadrons, to be formed at Neuburg on the Danube to watch Bernadotte and the Bavarians about Bamberg; a flying column of 4 battalions, 2 squadrons, then moving from Bohemia on Amberg was to act as vanguard to the chief command. Kienmayer's Corps had been delayed on the way, *but was now ordered to bring up the troops on country carriages*[6] *and accelerate its movement by every means in its power.*

---

6. Napoleon's expedient of sending the Imperial Guard to the front in horsed carriages in 1806 was therefore anticipated by Mack.

All the troops in Tyrol were ordered in to Bavaria, and steps were actually taken to transfer 20,000 men from the Army of Italy to Mack's command; these however were never carried out, and other orders were issued, which brought the Austrian forces on the 3rd October into the following positions:

Jellacic's Corps. Wolfkeel's Brigade, 5 battalions, 6 squadrons (3000 men), at Lindau, Tettnang, Buchhorn, Merseburg; Richter's Brigade, 7 battalions (3500), Achberg, Wangen, Isny, and towards Kempten; the remainder gathering at Feldkirch.

Schwartzenberg's Corps. Main body (Gottesheim) at Ravensburg, Mengen, to Sigmaringen, Markdorf (8600).

Klenau's Command Advance Guard and Reserve. Advance guard, 1 battalion rifles, 14 squadrons at Pfullendorf-Stokach, Engen and Radolfzell; Reserve, 8 squadrons (Mack's) Cuirassiers at Wurzach, and 4 battalions Grenadiers at Biberach and Waldsee (5000 men).

Riesch's Corps. headquarters Weissenhorn, and generally distributed between the Iller and Lech. Gyulai, Kerpen and Hesse-Homburg along the Danube, with Auffenberg on the march from the Tyrol between Memmingen-Wertingen and Burgau (30,000 men).

Werneck's Corps. headquarters Türkheim. Hohenzollerns' Division, Buchloe, Türkheim-Mindelheim (6500).

Kienmayer's Corps. 1 battalion and headquarters Munich; 3 at Neuburg, 3 battalions and 16 squadrons Ingolstadt, 8 squadrons Eichstadt, 4 squadrons near Ellwangen, 2 squadrons towards Amberg with reserves still on the march.

As a preparatory deployment, the enemy being supposed still at a distance, and cantonments being largely conditioned by positions of magazines in Austrian enclaves, it is not easy to find fault with this distribution. The troops covered a rectangle, about 100 miles by 60 square, and could be concentrated for action without forced marching, facing either west or north within about seventy-two hours, and, the neutrality of Ansbach being assumed, it will be seen that the

Austrians were in a position to turn with their whole force on either of the enemy's columns as best might suit their purpose. In fact they were on "interior lines" to the French Columns, as they had a right to believe these columns to be moving. They could leave a retaining force behind field entrenchments on the Iller to gain time against the main French columns, and then turn upon Bernadotte and the Bavarians, or vice versa detain Bernadotte whilst turning on Napoleon.

Whatever reason those who had fought against the French in 1796, in the same theatre of war, might have to fear the consequence of an encounter against a numerically superior force, Mack himself with the memories of his victories in Belgium had no particular reason to flinch from such a venture.

Moreover, he was not there pledged to win a decisive battle or perish, but merely to gain time and to hold the French until the Russians could reach the Inn, and the wider he made his zone of manoeuvres obviously the more opportunities he would find for delaying his enemy.

That Napoleon's columns could outmarch him by nearly two miles to one was an idea that could not in reason have entered his head. Nothing in previous experience existed to justify such an assumption, and if the idea did perhaps for a moment flash across his mind, the results of his own experiment in forcing men beyond the normal rate of movement could only cause him hope that his enemy would be so ill advised as to make the attempt; for in this rapid advance to the Iller, the Austrian Army, hastily got together, had fallen into lamentable disarray. Half-trained horses had died by the dozen, ill-fitting harness had used up many more, stragglers had multiplied exceedingly, and the whole Army was sorely in need of the rest it now expected to get, but of which it was so soon to be robbed.

After the event, all the hardships of this march were remembered against Mack, and he was asked why he had hurried them on so remorselessly. His answer, however, was conclusive, and may as well be cited at once:

> The Lech could be turned as easily as the Iller, the line of the Isar was untenable, hence only the Inn remained, and if this had been held half the Army would have been needed to close the roads through the Tyrol. But some 30,000 men would have been altogether too few to stop the united onset of the whole French Army, and from the Inn to Vienna there is not room enough to gain time. Hence the Austrians would be beaten, and the French reach Vienna before the Russians could come to its assistance.

There remained thus only the district between the Iller and Lech as a zone for concentration, and orders having been given to accumulate magazines at Ulm, Memmingen, and elsewhere, Mack really was as well justified in selecting Ulm as a temporary base as was Napoleon in choosing Dresden for the same purpose in 1813. Indeed he was more so; for if the enemy closed in on him as the Allies did on Dresden, he could always march out across his communications on the left bank of the Danube and join the Russians; whilst if they pressed on him from the north he could retire on any point of his base, which extended from the Inn along the Tyrolese frontier, and was extended by Lake Constance and the Rhine at least as far as Schaffhausen.

The ultimate cause of his downfall must be looked for far deeper than in the man or the Army alone. *It was fundamentally the want of a real national spirit as driving force to the Army which was lacking.* Had there been representatives of the people with guillotines on travelling carriages to enforce obedience to Mack's orders—those orders to which the Archduke Charles took twenty foolscap pages of exception—the result of the campaign might have been very different.

Chapter 4

The March from Boulogne to the Rhine

In the previous chapter I have sketched out the manner in which Austria was gradually inveigled into a fighting coalition against the French, and the nature of her preparations to meet the first shocks of the coming war.

Few of these details escaped the notice of Napoleon's secret agents, but for want of the key to their inner significance he paid little attention to them until the beginning of August 1805, when, in view of the dilatoriness and want of enterprise of his Admirals and his Spanish Allies, it became apparent to him that his chances of being allowed by the Continent of Europe to carry through his projected invasion of England were becoming exceedingly precarious.

From the moment of rupture of the Treaty of Amiens he had of course anticipated that Great Britain would exert every conceivable means of raising the Continent against him, but had considered himself safeguarded against such endeavours primarily by the factor of *time*, and secondly by the seizure of Hanover, and the use he intended to make of its possession in his dealings with Prussia.

He had by this time thoroughly grasped the innate selfishness of the old diplomacy, based, as I have before explained, on the view then held by all kings and princes by divine right, that the land they ruled over was in fact their property in the same sense as a great landowner regards his estate in the present day viz. a trust to be developed and handed on to his descendants by every means that the legal ingenuity of his solicitors can contrive. The Chancelleries and diplomatists stood to their kings in the same relation that old family solicitors stood to their employers, and identified themselves with all royal interests in much the same manner believing it to be their duty to remember that the estate never dies, and to protect its interests against possible temporary aberrations of the proprietor for the time being.

Thus Prussia coveted Hanover, while Austrian and Prussian interests were in direct opposition to one another in Poland, and at many other points. Austria could hardly fight Prussia single-handed; hence, if Prussia could be induced to ally herself with France in exchange for Hanover, no amount of intrigue on the part of Russia would suffice to force Austria into the field.

Therefore immediately after the seizure of Hanover negotiations were opened with Prussia, in which the latter was offered the reversion of Hanover, on the conclusion of peace, in exchange for a treaty of alliance with France .The Prussian Foreign Office rose readily to the bait. But like sound men of business, realising the importance of the advantages already held, they began bargaining for the best terms they could obtain. Being above all things anxious to keep the peace of Europe, at any rate north of the Alps, they proposed that Napoleon should join them in guaranteeing the neutrality of the Southern German States. This however was entirely unacceptable to Napoleon because, as he pointed out to the Prussian Ambassador in Paris, Luchesini (November 1803), it not only left the Austrians free to attack him in Italy, but deprived him of the very roads by which he could most directly deliver a counter-attack in the event of hostilities on the Italian frontier. Further proposals were then put forward, and much time was lost in their consideration; but nothing the French could do would induce the King of Prussia to sanction the use of the word "Alliance" in any of the proposed treaties. In fact he could not honourably do so, because all the time that his agents were negotiating with France he himself was corresponding privately with the Emperors of Austria and Russia.

Meanwhile rumours of Austrian war preparations continued to reach Napoleon, who desired his Ambassador in Vienna, La Rochefoucauld, to obtain explanations, which were duly furnished to the following effect.

Owing to the spread of yellow fever introduced into Italy from the West Indies, the Austrian Government had found itself compelled to guard its frontiers against the disease by establishing a cordon of troops, and these having been moved out of their cantonments, it had been found necessary to bring up others from the interior to take the places thus left vacant. The troops moved had been almost exclusively infantry and only some. 18,000 in number. This statement being confirmed by the Emperor of Austria in his own handwriting, in a very straightforward reply to a letter addressed directly to him by Napoleon, the latter for the moment accepted the explanation as satisfactory. He however wrote again to say that he was so anxious to avoid any possibilities of misunderstandings in the future, that he proposed to unite the Italian Republics then under French dominion into an independent kingdom which should act as a buffer-state between the two nations, but he did not state his intentions, already formed, of placing the Iron Crown of the new kingdom upon his own head.

This correspondence took place during December 1803 and January 1804, and for the moment did much to strengthen the hands of the peace party. Napoleon's negotiations and assurances to Russia were equally satisfactory, and indeed the War Party in the latter Empire were hard pressed to find an excuse for the hostilities so eagerly desired. Hence the news of Napoleon's coronation at Milan, followed immediately by his incorporation of Genoa into the new kingdom, came as a positive godsend to further the ambitions of the War Party.

The seizure of Genoa in particular affected Russian interests, and decisively won over the Emperor Alexander to the War Party, while the two events together convinced both Emperors that peace with France could never be maintained as long as her affairs were in Napoleon's hands. This view of the matter seems never to have struck Napoleon himself, who for the time being devoted himself entirely to home affairs and the prosecution of his designs against Great Britain. How thoroughly in earnest he was as regards the latter seems to me conclusively established by the fact that he took no steps whatever to buy horses for transport or to organise supply trains until a few days before he commenced his great march to the Rhine.

The only precautionary measures he adopted to meet the possibilities which the reports of his secret agents all over Europe continued to foreshadow with increasing intensity was to open a correspondence with the courts of Bavaria, Würtemberg and Baden with a view to obtaining contingents from them, and facilities of movement through their dominions. These bear the stamp of carelessness, very unusual in anything emanating from his mind, as the following example will show.

His first idea of Bavarian co-operation was the suggestion that a Corps of 20,000 men (i.e. practically the whole Bavarian Army) should take up a position about Passau to dispute the passage of the Inn against the Austrians. Let the reader look at the map and note the line of the Inn in relation to the Tyrol, all of which district was held by the Austrians. I think he will agree with the Bavarian generals, who one and all refused to accept the responsibility of such a command, because it was certain to lead to an unconditional surrender in the open field. For once Napoleon did not insist, but left the Bavarians free to make their own dispositions.

Since the trend of all the reports he received throughout the summer pointed unmistakably to hostilities in the very near future, it is presumable that he still relied absolutely on being able to buy the Prussian Alliance when it became worth his while to offer what he believed to be a full price for it *viz*. Hanover unconditionally. In this he would probably have been right had he only had the Prussian Foreign Office to deal with. But he did not know, and apparently did not even suspect, how the King had already pledged himself to the Emperor Alexander and the Court of Vienna.

When, therefore, from the reports he received between the 12th and 21st of August (in particular one from Strasburg, dated 21st, stating that the Austrians were giving out contracts and filling up magazines in Suabia), he decided to declare war against Austria, and thereby renounced all his schemes against England. He forthwith despatched Duroc, as a special plenipotentiary, to sign and seal the alliance he desired in return for his immediate surrender of Hanover, the garrison of which country *viz*. Bernadotte's Corps of some 20,000 men he intended to employ more profitably elsewhere, a point which the Prussians could hardly have overlooked.

The letter Duroc took with him was frankness personified, and deserves reproduction as one of the most characteristic from Napoleon's pen.

> Camp of Boulogne
> 23rd August, 1805
> *My Brother*,
> I am sending to your Majesty General Duroc. He is provided with full powers to sign, with the individual your Majesty is pleased to designate, the treaty on which our Ministers have agreed. I rejoice at the new bonds which will draw together our States. We have enemies in common. The acquisition of Hanover is a geographical necessity to your Majesty, particularly when Europe

is divided between such great Powers. The partition of Poland has brought about a great change; it has cancelled Sweden and made Russia a European Power to which there is no adequate counterpoise, for Constantinople and Ispahan no longer count. Austria redoubles her preparations; the Elector of Bavaria is much alarmed. Your Majesty has not a day to lose in ordering a concentration on your Bohemian frontier. I have ordered the whole of my correspondence with Austria to be communicated to your Majesty; if she does not order her troops back into their peace quarters I am determined to march at the head of more than 100,000 men into Bavaria, and we shall have to fight again. God, my conscience, your Majesty, and Europe will be my witnesses that I am attacked, since I am menaced on my frontiers when my troops are on board my ships or on the coast. The House of Austria is in no position to make head against me. She is wilfully blind. The evils of war will fall upon her. I have nothing to fear from this struggle, with, however, the help of God from whom all things depend. My Brother, a new scene is about to present itself to Europe. It is necessary that we should come to an understanding and work in harmony for the repose of the world and the good of our countries. I flatter myself that neither your Majesty or I will fail, and that we shall leave our dominions, and those of the princes who make common cause with us, in the same splendour to which they have at present attained. I have spared the House of Austria too much; she is still too powerful to leave Europe at rest and not to attempt to undermine the liberties of Germany. If she remains armed war is imminent. Every opportunity which may arise to give proofs of my esteem and friendship will be moments of happiness for me.

Napoleon

What the inevitable effect of such a letter upon a monarch by right Divine must be, it is evident that he never paused to think, for on the very day of its despatch, his last hopes of a successful termination to Villeneuve's manoeuvres having vanished, he began issuing orders for the march to the Rhine.

His first step was to write to Dejean, Minister of Administration for War, to order 500,000 rations of biscuit at Strassburg, and 200,000 at Mayence (Corres. No. 9122), and the Inspector General of Artillery sent out circulars to the Directors of Artillery at Strasburg, Mayence, Metz, and Neuf Breisach to have all the rolling material in their several charges prepared immediately for the field.[1] Marmont was warned to be ready to disembark his troops from the transports at short notice, and Bernadotte was directed to assemble his Corps at Gottingen in view of hostilities with Austria. On the 24th August Berthier issued instructions for various preparatory movements for units other than those already incorporated in the Grand Army to facilitate the final concentration on the Rhine.

Berthier's letter to Marmont deserves citation, as it shows that there was still a lingering hesitation in the Emperor's mind.

> I would warn you, General, that the Emperor's squadron sailed from Ferrol in company with the Spaniards on the 14th August. If these combined squadrons arrive in the channel, the Emperor will immediately undertake the expedition to England; but if, by reason either of adverse winds or of want of audacity in our admirals, they do not reach the channel, the Emperor and King will adjourn the expedition to another year. . . . But I must advise you that in the present state of affairs in Europe, the Emperor will be obliged to disperse the assemblies of Austrian troops in Tyrol hence it is his Majesty's intention that you should be ready on receipt of

1. On the same day a letter was received from De Songis in reply to an inquiry by Berthier, dated the 20th inst., stating that no trace could be found of any stores of harness in their arsenal.

further orders from me to disembark and march your command towards Mayence, giving out that the troops are moving into cantonments, and keeping the secret of their destination as long as possible.

On the 24th August the Cuirassiers and Dragoons are directed on the Rhine and their organisation modified. Four Cuirassier Regiments from the interior (*i.e.* not belonging to the "Army of England") are ordered to Landau to make up a Division under d'Hautpoul, whilst that of Nansouty marches from Lille to Schlettstadt and Neuf Breisach. The two enormous Divisions of Dragoons, one of 9, the other of 11 regiments, are broken up, and by the addition of 4 other regiments from the interior are formed into 4 Divisions of 2 brigades each of 3 regiments, and sent to watch the Rhine from Schlettstadt to Spire, all possible precautions being taken to keep their destinations secret. On the next day the Dragoons and Oudinot's Grenadiers are warned to march "to-morrow," the 26th, and their destination is no longer limited by the Rhine, but may extend along the road from Strassburg to Vienna, into Bavaria. Evidently they were intended as an Advance Guard on which the Bavarians could rally.

So far the Emperor seems to have had no doubt that he would be able to reach the Inn undisturbed, since in his instructions to Murat and Bertrand, despatched to reconnoitre on the 25th August, he directs their attention particularly to the country between the Lech and the Inn and beyond. They were to call at Würzburg and Ulm respectively on their way and report upon each place as points of support to a line of communications, but not with a view to tactical operations in their vicinity.

On the 26th August the Emperor dictated the orders of march for the Corps of Davout, Soult, Lannes and Ney. The latter was directed on Schlettstadt, Soult and Lannes to Strassburg, Davout to Hagenau. Marmont was to march on

Mayence, where he was to arrive about the 15th September, and Bernadotte was ordered to Gottingen, both the latter being warned that they would probably have to continue their march on Würzburg.

The heads of the Columns had hardly begun to march when the Emperor suddenly changed their destinations. On the 28th August he wrote to Dejean:

> Landau will be one of the chief points of assembly. I have told you to have 500,000 rations of biscuit at Strassburg; it will be convenient to divide them as follows, 200,000 Strassburg, 200,000 at Landau, 100,000 at Spire.

Under this new disposition Davout, Soult and Ney were to lie between Hagenau and Spire, and only the Advance Guard was to remain near Strassburg, while Savary was sent out the same day to reconnoitre three lines of road starting from Carlsruhe and ending on the Danube between Ulm and Dillingen.

The explanation generally accepted of this sudden change in Napoleon's dispositions is that by this step the troops avoided the difficult defiles of the Black Forest, and were better placed to execute the manoeuvres which ultimately ended in the surrender of Mack at Ulm.

But as the French *Official History* of the campaign points out, it is nothing less than puerile to suggest that Napoleon only heard for the first time of the difficulties of the Black Forest between the 27th and 28th August, or could have planned the manoeuvre of Ulm at a time when he had not the remotest reason to suppose that Mack intended to go there.

Up to the night of the 27th all that the French Emperor knew of the Austrian preparations was that they were in progress at various points along the frontier, and he believed that by keeping the movement of his own troops secret, and using all possible speed, he could anticipate them between the Lech and the Inn. But during that night he appears to have learnt that both the Austrian and Russian preparations were much further advanced than he had believed them to be, and as it was 400 miles from the coast to the Rhine, and only 300 from the Rhine to the Inn, it suddenly appeared quite possible that the Austrians would reach the Rhine first, in which case the concentration of his whole army before collision ensued in the positions first indicated would be doubtful if not impossible.

Everything pointed to the march of the Austrians by the shortest and for them most convenient roads through Ulm to Strassburg, Memmingen and Freiburg, on which he already knew they had accumulated provisions. The revised orders therefore rendered his concentration on his left secure, and in his further advance on Ulm and Dillingen he preserved full freedom of manoeuvre either against the Austrians to the south or the Russians from Bohemia should they elect to come that way; and in case of necessity he could change his base from Mayence and Strassburg to Strassburg and Neuf Breisach, as circumstances might dictate.

The Grand Army

The great weakness of the Grand Army as it stood on the shores of the channel, its units duly assigned to their respective brigades, divisions and corps, lay in the want of an adequate General Staff to combine and co-ordinate its movements. There were indeed a considerable number of war experienced men accustomed to the office work of the field, excellent as individuals, but not trained in the same school to view matters from the same standpoint, or to work in harmony with one another, and even these were insufficient in number, whilst no arrangements whatever existed for the education and subsequent selection of men to fill its junior ranks. In default of such a school, selection tempered by favouritism produced a plentiful crop of typical "brass hats"—*i.e.* men who, insufficiently taught to appreciate the true needs and capacity of the soldiers in the ranks, issue orders which can only be obeyed at the expense of the fighting efficiency of the troops, or circulate them with such carelessness that they generally arrive too late at their destination. Such types were not unknown in the British Army during the first months of Lord Roberts' South African Campaign.

The actual composition of the army as regards rank and file was excellent. From the inspection returns preserved in the archives, it appears that 50,538 out of 115,582 had already seen service, though this number was very unevenly distributed amongst the different arms. The Sappers coming first with 77 per cent, of their strength, then the Light Cavalry and the Infantry averaging 42.5 per cent.

The number of men over 10 years of service varied considerably. In the 17th Line there were 918 out of 951, in the 13th Light Infantry 540 out of 569, and the 14th Line came lowest with 267 out of 741. Generally 25 per cent of the Army had fought all through the campaigns of the Republic, a second quarter had been through Marengo or Hohenlinden, and the remainder had been enlisted since 1801.

Nearly all the officers and non-commissioned officers had seen service, and in each regiment there were still some sturdy survivors of the old Royal Army, some with 40 years' service.

The Hussars had been the most conservative, and retained most of their old traditions; they had received very few conscripts, but had kept up their numbers by voluntary enlistments, generally from Alsatian or other German families. One half of their officers were however quite illiterate, and many did not even know the words of command in French. Marbot's description of them as they were in 1799 was still substantially accurate in 1805, they remained soldiers first and troubled themselves not at all about political questions.

The other arms had absorbed the republican spirit, tempered by an iron despotism in face of the enemy. Off parade they might argue as they pleased, in action obedience was absolute, but on the march a betwixt and between system was observed, and straggling and marauding, as the sequel will show, soon reached terrible proportions. Each regiment had its own traditions, and the wretched recruits were hazed and bullied unmercifully until they conformed. Hence desertion during the Camp was very high, from 5 to 8 per cent, per annum, but all this vanished when on the march to the Rhine. The men were freely given furlough on their honour to rejoin at their final destination, and only some forty men in Soult's Corps failed to appear before the river was crossed. The complaints, however, against the want of physical development in the recruits were ceaseless, though as yet the drain on the population had not been at all serious. But these complaints are common to every army in which *esprit de corps* runs high, and since these men did in fact accomplish perhaps the fastest and furthest march in history under the heaviest floods and over some of the worst of roads, they must be taken more as an indication of the pride of the Army than as an evidence of real shortcoming in the recruits themselves.

The composition of the officers present with the Grand Army is of peculiar interest. The total number was 5000; of these about 100 came from the new school for officers at Fontainebleau, and were between 17 and 21 years of age, 500 to 600 from the original volunteers of 1792 or from the conscripts raised since the commencement of the Revolution. These were mostly picked men, selected for their general standard of instruction and social position, like de Fezensac, or for distinguished conduct in action, as Dulong, commanding a battalion at twenty-five; but mostly they were still lieutenants in 1805. The remainder had all served with the old Royal Army either in the ranks, or as officers had survived the general debacle.

The average age of the sub-lieutenants was 32, and that of the lieutenants 37, whilst those of the Captains and superior regimental officers was only 39; but there were more than ninety lieutenants over 50 years of age, and four over 60.

> Men were already beginning to grumble in the Grand Army, and it looks as if a few more years of peace would have destroyed it. This is not its only fault. It is very poorly trained to manoeuvres, almost all the old professional officers of the old Royal Army have disappeared, and the few who remain have attained high rank, whence they exercise little influence on the instruction of their men, and drill has become exceedingly neglected.[2]

This, by the way, almost inevitably happens in an Army which has grown up on the Battlefield, and fought with almost constant success. Men feel that they are "good enough" and, having never felt the need of iron discipline in disaster, object to what they consider merely unpractical playing at soldiers.

It is the school of defeat that in the long run turns out the better fighting men and leaders, and hence the curious swing of the pendulum that has so often occurred between races of approximately equal fighting capacity. The recruits were supposed to be drilled at the depots, but, as usual, all the most infirm and useless officers had been relegated to these positions, and the instruction given appears to have been very indifferent indeed.

The Cavalry were poorly mounted, and only here and there in the confidential returns is an officer mentioned as showing keenness or knowledge of equitation, proving how low the standard had fallen since former days.

Next to the Hussars, the Artillery and Engineers had suffered least from the Revolution. The Artillery remained to the last the elite of the whole Army, but the Engineers as a body seem to have been about the standard of our military foremen of works, good at estimating and at the drawing board, but with no broad grasp of the principles of their profession.

2. Vol. i. p. 179.

The analysis of the ages and service of the 141 General Officers is very interesting. Their ages vary from one of 29 years to one of 58, but the mean is 40. One quarter had served as officers of the old army, one quarter in its ranks, and the remainder came chiefly from the levies subsequent to 1791. That is to say that the men sprung from the great upheaval of that year had been on the whole more successful in their career than the older professional officers, some 4000 of whom were still in regimental positions.

The most crying need of the Army, however, was horses, both for Cavalry, Artillery and transport. Many Dragoons, in fact, were organised in dismounted battalions and marched to the front on their own feet, trusting to pick up horses by the way, and for transport only one contract was given out in May, when possibilities of an Austrian campaign were first in sight. This was made with the "Compagnie Breidt" for the provision of 30 brigades of wagons, of which however only 6, with 163 wagons, were actually ready in time.[3]

Nothing to my mind could indicate more clearly than these deficiencies the reality of Napoleon's determination to invade England, for no transports, and but little cavalry and artillery, would be needed for a march upon London, hence few were provided. But had the intention only been to prepare an army at Boulogne for employment anywhere in Europe at large, it is contrary to everything we know of the Emperor's methods to imagine it destitute of the chief conditions favouring the mobility he relied on so thoroughly and so well knew how to direct.

Nevertheless, whatever the shortcomings in tactical training, organisation, and so forth, disclosed in the above pages, we have generally been led to believe that such as it was the Grand Army crossed the Rhine, ready to the last gaiter button, horse and foot.

---

3. See *Studien zur Kriegsgeschichte und Taktik*, part üi., note, p. 13. General Staff, Berlin.

Nothing, however, could well have been further from the truth, for the records now published reveal deficiencies many times greater than those which sufficed to paralyse the Imperial Army during the latter days of July 1870, and one is often tempted to wonder what might have been the fate of the German Armies in the Palatinate had Napoleon I., not his nephew, Napoleon III., been in supreme command at that date.

The march across had been almost as trying as in an enemy's country, for, though countless orders to secure adequate preparations along the several roads chosen for the movement had been sent on in advance, neither time or money was forthcoming to ensure their execution. On the whole the men fared well at least they received enough to eat and generally a roof to sleep under. But the civil population, particularly in the north, was by no means anxious to help them. The Mayors would assign billets in villages four or five miles away from the main roads, thus adding materially to the fatigue of the men, who already were timed at an average of nearly twenty miles a day, and when the town of Lille absolutely refused to receive the 1st Division of the III. Corps, Davout took the law into his own hands and forthwith quartered his men on the inhabitants as in an enemy's country.

At Vitry too, the troops having consented to sleep in the empty barracks if straw was provided, the town failed to provide the straw, and when the officers complained the mayor refused to furnish the marching-out certificates of good conduct, which each marching unit was by law compelled to obtain. The bad roads in the Ardennes also played havoc with the shoe leather and many units reached the Rhine almost shoeless.

As usual, however, the horses suffered far the most. Forage was scarce, and often green, and neither men nor horses were in sufficient condition for long marches, hence sore backs were frequent, many horses broke down altogether, and had to be left at the depots along the road.

The Artillery suffered in particular, and Soult reported a deficiency of 400 in his Corps when it arrived at its destination, and as these were not made good when the passage of the Rhine began, he was compelled to leave his ammunition wagons behind.

Davout suffered equally, being obliged to abandon even some of his guns. Probably he preferred to take fewer complete units fully supplied with ammunition rather than risk finding such artillery as he had useless for want of it.

Only open country carts were available for the Infantry ammunition, and as a consequence between 200,000 and 300,000 rounds were rendered useless by bad weather and had to be left behind.

But hard cash was the chief necessity, for the contractors refused to deliver even such goods as they had ready until they had received a big percentage of their price, and many units entered the campaign deficient of boots, great-coats and other necessities of equipment which it is the custom to consider essential.

Fortunately pay for the troops was issued for a fortnight in advance before German territory was entered, and no doubt the men and officers did what they could to supply their immediate needs.

The army transport was in the worst case of all, for, except for the wagons supplied by the Compagnie Breidt, it had to rely exclusively on country carts of the most primitive description drawn by requisitioned horses and men, and the latter deserted freely whenever opportunity arose, taking their horses with them when they could. Soult could only get together 700 horses out of the 1200 he required, and on 1st October he reports that 300 had already disappeared. The vacancies thus caused had to be filled by requisition along the line of march through Baden and Würtemberg, and this proceeding was most bitterly resented by the inhabitants. By the time the concentration was finished the

Cavalry was practically starving for lack of money to buy such forage as the country still contained, and had to cross the river forthwith in order to take it from the people they came in theory to protect.

Marmont, coming down the Rhine from Holland, was in no better case; indeed, in some respects he was worse off than the others, for many of his cavalry and artillery horses had been cooped up for some time on board the ships waiting to cross over into England. Agents were sent on in advance to purchase horses along the Rhine, but, as in Alsace, people were not very anxious to complete their contracts, and much of his material had to be sent on by water and left at Mayence until there was water enough in the Main to forward them on to Würzburg.

The orders sent to Bernadotte in Hanover directed him to move to Würzburg by the shortest line, but they were delayed in transition, and Bernadotte, whose position in the midst of a hostile population was already sufficiently precarious, had already arranged for a free passage through the territories of the Elector of Hesse-Cassel to Frankfurt, on the ground that the Corps was ordered to rejoin at Strassburg by the shortest line.

The Elector conceded his request for thirty-five days only, but, probably under Prussian influence, withdrew the concession before this period had nearly run off, and whilst the heavy baggage of the Corps was still on Hanoverian territory. The head of Bernadotte's Corps was already nearing Frankfurt by the Fulda road from the north, when his orders to proceed at once to Würzburg reached him, and at the same time came a notice that Frankfurt and its resources were reserved for Marmont. He at once bent off for the valley of the Main by cross-roads to Aschaffenburg, and ultimately reached Würzburg, with his troops so worn out that the Corps had to be granted a three days' rest. In Würzburg itself they found nothing of the biscuits, stores, etc., which had been ordered in advance.

No wonder when the Emperor reached the front at Strassburg (25th September) he was "little satisfied by the state in which he found the supply and transport services of the Army" (vol. ii. p. 10).

Duroc in the meanwhile had reached Berlin, where he soon discovered how serious were the difficulties and how many the delays which must intervene before Prussia would consent to the Emperor's proposals. On the 8th September he wrote at length to his master, diplomatically hinting that as a road led out of the main valley from a point to the north of Würzburg leading to Bamberg, it would be well to instruct Bernadotte to proceed along it, as it avoided all Prussian territories. This was as near a warning of dangers ahead as Duroc could safely venture to administer to a ruler as impatient of advice as was Napoleon. It also is of special interest since it is clear it would not have been written had not the intention to violate the territory of Ausbach—*i.e.* of Prussia—been already a matter of common knowledge to the inner circle of the Court before Duroc's departure.

The warning letter arrived during the night of the 17th September, and its perusal brought on one of those rare fits of rage to which the Emperor is reported to have given way. This fact is worth dwelling upon because it helps to reveal so much of the working of the Imperial mind, and almost guarantees the honesty of his convictions at the moment when he wrote the letter to the King of Prussia which I have cited above.

It was the first psychological moment of the coming campaign, marking the first serious disillusionment as to his capacity to read aright the riddle of his adversaries' policy. For the time he found himself between the horns of a dilemma. Either he adhered to his original resolutions, and Bernadotte marched through Ansbach at the risk of adding the still unshaken Prussian Army (180,000 men) to the lists of the Emperor's foes, and opening up strategical possibilities to his enemies which so far at least had never entered into his original calculations; or he followed Duroc's indication, and thereby compelled himself to risk a concentration within striking distance of Mack, whose numerical strength he still overrated by 20 per cent.

His decision, contained in an order to Bernadotte, despatched the same day (17th), directing him to march through Ausbach, seems to me to prove how strongly he was affected by the imminence of the second danger which jeopardised the success of the campaign from the beginning; whereas the former evils required time to develop, and might be averted by the rapid and victorious advance of his forces as indeed they were. Of the real nature of the struggle within his own mind his letters contain no trace; on the contrary, both to Talleyrand, Murat and Otto, his *charge d'affaires* with the Bavarians, he wrote in his most enthusiastic vein. But this is a characteristic of his whole correspondence: the greater the actual danger, the more he encourages his subordinates to take a rosy view of things, and, speaking generally, his despatches on the eve of great events bear no more relation to the actual facts of the situation than, let us say, the remarks of an American financier to an interviewer on the morning of the day he absconds with all his available assets, and the motive is the same in both cases *viz.* to keep up confidence amongst one's subordinates to the last possible moment.

Thus on the 27th September, when the state of his transport, and mounted services generally, must have caused him the gravest apprehensions he writes to Bernadotte:

> The Emperor of Germany makes no detachment on the right hand of the Danube,[4] the Russians have not yet arrived. I am ready to meet everything. . . . If only the Austrians remain asleep for the next three or four days on the Iller and in the Black Forest, I shall have turned them, and I hope only the debris will escape.

---

4. *Campagne de 1805.* Vol. ü., p. 35.

This prediction is so far in advance of anything which the facts actually in his possession justified him in assuming, and the wording is so careless, admitting of several interpretations, that one can only regard it as intended to hearten up its recipient in view of the consequences which he doubtless foresaw were likely to follow the violation of Ansbach territories which Bernadotte was ordered to carry out.

Chapter 5

From the Rhine to the Danube

Under normal circumstances, at this season of the year, the march before the Grand Army presented no particular difficulties. The rise from the Rhine Valley to the watersheds of the Neckar and Danube was not excessive, and beyond, the descent over rolling downs and through fertile plains in which the harvest had only just been gathered seemed to suit the new spirit of French operations to the utmost. Even the steep and somewhat barren transverse barrier of the Rauhe Alp, a continuation of the Jura Mountains running from Schaffhausen, past Ulm transversely across the line of advance, was as nothing to what French troops had frequently had to deal with in previous years.

Unfortunately, the weather changed everything. Instead of the beautiful Indian summer which usually ushers in October in these districts, the month broke cold and inclement. Rain, sleet, and even snow pelted down incessantly, and soon the roads became mere watercourses and the fields veritable quagmires. Fezensac's graphic description will complete the picture.

> This short campaign proved to me a foretaste of all those others which were to come afterwards. The extremity of fatigue, the want of food, the terrible weather, the trouble of the marauders—nothing was wanting, and in one month I tasted a sample of what was to be my des-

tiny during the whole of my career. The brigades, even the regiments were sometimes dispersed, the order to reunite arrived late, because it had to filter through so many offices. Hence the troops were marching day and night, and I saw for the first time men sleeping as they marched. I could not have believed it possible. Thus we reached our destination without having eaten anything and finding nothing to eat. It was all very well for Berthier to write: 'In the war of invasion as the Emperor makes it, there are no magazines; it is for the Generals to provide themselves from the country as they traverse it'; but the Generals had neither time or means to procure regularly what was required for the needs of such a numerous Army. This order was an authorisation of pillage, and the districts we passed through suffered cruelly. We were often hungry, and the terrible weather intensified our sufferings. A steady cold rain or rather half-melted snow fell incessantly, and we stumbled along in the cold mud churned by our passage almost up to our knees the wind made it impossible to light fires.

On the 16th of October the weather was so infamous that not a soul remained at his post. One found neither sentries nor pickets, even the Artillery remained unguarded, every one sought shelter as best he could, and never again, except in Russia, did I see the army suffer so much or in such disorder.

*****

All these causes developed insubordination and thieves. When in such weather the troops entered a village, it was hard to get them out again hence the number of stragglers roaming about the country became considerable. The inhabitants were exposed to ill treatment of all descriptions; and the wounded officers left behind, who tried to assert their authority, were openly defied and threatened by the marauders. All these details are unknown to those who read the history of our campaign, one sees only a valiant army whose soldiers vie with their officers for glory, and the price of suffering paid for the most brilliant successes is forgotten.

In circumstances such as the above no one man's testimony can ever be taken as conclusive, more especially when written many years after the event one's personal impressions are too liable to be influenced by any passing affliction. What seems to a man suffering from fever, and the terrible depression that so often accompanies it, as the very limit of human misery, passes unnoticed by his comrade, for the time being, in the enjoyment of perfect health and physical vigour; and there are always enough invalids still struggling through their duties in any Army to supply material enough for the darkest pictures of human suffering. But in this case de Fezensac receives abundant confirmation from the letters of the French generals published in the official history of the campaign.

The whole army, as we have seen, crossed the Rhine seriously short of transport and biscuit, and complaints began to reach the Emperor from the very first, for on the 7th October he issued an order reminding the superior commanders that "one should always have four days' bread in reserve"; but the order did not materially improve matters, as the following extracts sufficiently show:[1]

On the 9th of October General Bouvier writes:

It is with the utmost difficulty that my Division has so far been able to provide itself with subsistence. For several days they have had neither bread nor meat, and only most scanty supplies of forage, particularly of oats. The villages I have had to occupy have been completely cleared out by preceding columns.

1. For originals see *La Campagne de 1805*. Introduction, vol. iii., p. 5 et seq.

The same day Suchet was still able to issue bread to his Division (thanks no doubt to the measures taken by Soult, his Corps Commander); but the remaining Divisions of his Corps (the IV.), from his own report, had to go without, and worn out by the awful weather had to halt at Augsburg to receive two days' rations. Vandamme wrote:

> The troops are exhausted by fatigue and suffer particularly from want of food. It is most urgent that we should at last receive some issue of provisions.

Fortunately a convoy of 4000 rations and a magazine of corn and oats fell into their hands about the following day. On the same date (9th October) Marmont also wrote:

> The troops would have marched at once and should have slept at Pornbach if the cruel hunger from which they suffer had not rendered it indispensable to halt, in order to distribute to them some provisions. They are to receive a third of a ration of bread and some potatoes, after which they will resume their march and, I hope, make good 9 miles on the road to Pfaffenhofen.

Next day, the 10th October, he writes to Berthier:

> I have the honour to recall to your recollection our want of food; it is extreme.

This state of destitution in which most of the Corps at this date found themselves does not appear to have astonished the Emperor, for in answer to Marmont's complaints Berthier writes on the 11th October:

> In all the letters which M. le General writes to me he speaks of 'provisions.' I must repeat to him that in the war of invasion now being prosecuted by the Emperor there are no magazines; it is the duty of the Generals commanding the Corps to provide themselves with immediate subsistence from the country they traverse. General

> Marmont has received the order to provide himself with four days' bread and biscuit in advance; he cannot therefore count on anything but the resources he can procure for himself, as all the other Corps of the Grand Army do likewise, and no one knows better than General Marmont the manner in which the Emperor makes war.

This letter deserves study, as it reveals in the clearest manner the *driving force* Napoleon knew how to apply. As M. Colin points out: "It would be indeed a difficult task to reconcile a satisfactory system of supply with the extreme mobility absolutely essential to the methods of the Grand Army"; but be this as it may, the fact remains that the extreme privations undergone by the troops brought in their train marauders, pillage and the break up of discipline.

Davout writes on the 11th October to Berthier:

> I have the honour to represent to your Excellency, that it has become absolutely necessary to take prompt measures to put a stop to marauding and pillaging, which have reached the limits of excess; the inhabitants of the district see with the keenest anguish that at the moment when their Prince and army are making common cause with us, they are receiving worse treatment than when allied with Austria against us—I have the honour to solicit your Excellency to procure for me the authority of his Majesty to shoot a few of these scoundrels—terrible examples are necessary to stop this evil, which is constantly growing.

To this letter no reply has been traced. It seems curious however to find this application for specific authority to make these necessary examples. This is a detail usually left to the discretion of a Corps Commander in the field, where punishment must of necessity be prompt if it is to be deterrent to others, and for the sake of the wretched Bavarian peasants one feels tempted to regret the absence of the "Representatives of the People" who in former campaigns would have made short work of these robbers.

The question then suggests itself whether it would have suited the Emperor's purpose to check this pillaging, whether in fact the probability of such occurrences had not already presented itself to his mind before the advance began.

If the men did not plunder it must have been clear that they could not live at the rate they were timed to march, and from 1796 the Emperor knew what an extraordinary spur to the marching power of his troops hunger, only to be satisfied by a forward movement and indiscriminate pillage, could prove. What matter if the inhabitants suffered and the weakly men amongst the troops fell out and died, if the remainder reached their destinations in time, for time was the all-important factor in the case, since it could not be reasonably foreseen how the weather was to play into the hands of the French. It is not a pleasant idea to contemplate, but it is necessary to bring it out in order to show how War in all its nakedness really appears to a clear-cut logical mind which refuses to consider anything but the most effective means to the end, and is troubled by no humanitarian sentimentality. To crush Mack finally and completely before the arrival of the Russians was the first and best hope of winning the campaign. It was therefore a justifiable economy of forces, to risk losing 20 per cent, of his men on the march in order to avert the probable protraction of the war by several battles and perhaps many months, which would have cost him far more in the end and when we come to compare the narrow margin of hours by which the Austrian combinations were defeated, one can only agree with the accuracy of his reasoning. Davout given a free hand could always keep order in his command by the sacrifice of time, therefore the power to keep order must be taken away from him, so that he should not be tempted to delay the forward movement.

The first itinerary for the march from the Rhine to the Danube was commenced on the 10th September, and aimed at the convergence of the several Corps by all available roads between Donauwörth and Ulm. Originally the start was fixed for the 1st October and date of arrival on the river for the 9th. Each Corps was allowed an area for requisitions extending to the left of its own road up to the next road on which troops were marching an arrangement which worked badly in practice, because the habit of bivouacking across the line of march in order to save the men unnecessary fatigue had become fixed in the French army, and not even an Imperial order would induce his subordinates to break with it.

The news of the Austrian advance to Ulm and the Iller, received on the 17th September, involved a small alteration in the general plan, Murat and Ney being now directed to skirt round Ulm by the roads through Rottenburg and Göppingen, reaching the Danube at Günzburg, and the Corps on the left sent lower down the river to Neuburg and Ingolstadt instead of Donauwörth; but no subsequent information was allowed to interfere in the general plan, and, except that the 25th September was fixed as the date of commencement, it may be considered that the basic order of the whole campaign was issued on the 20th of that month.

According to this document the troops were to move in the following order from right to left:

Murat, Ney, Lannes, the cavalry screen of the former pushed out well to the south, from Strassburgwa Rottenburg, Göppingen and Giengen to Günzburg. Ney, followed by the Imperial Guard, Carlsruhe, Pforzheim, Ludwigsburg, Aalen, Münster. Soult, from Speyer by Heilbronn and Nordlingen to Donauwörth. Davout, from Mannheim, Necker-Oelz, Ottingen, to Neuburg. Marmont, from Mayence by Aschaffenburg, Würzburg, Rothenburg-on-the-Tauber, through Ansbach territory, to Monheim and Neuburg). Bernadotte, from Frankfurt *via* Gemünden, Würzburg, Ansbach, Weissenburg, Ingolstadt. The

Bavarians from Bamberg through Nuremberg, and to follow Bernadotte from Weissenburg onwards; the heads of all Columns to march off simultaneously.

Again, however, human nature proved stronger than Imperial edicts, and the troops only began to move on the 26th, and then hardly as combatant units.

Murat's troops quickly picked up contact with Austrian light troops in the passes of the Black Forest, but these were so skilfully handled that the French failed altogether to take any prisoners. Whether as a consequence of the feeling of uncertainty thus induced, or for other reasons not to be traced, Lannes and the main body of Murat's Corps now left the road assigned to them through the Kniebis Pass and marched down the Rhine valley and through Rastatt to Pforzheim, where they came into collision with Ney's columns and changed their order, Lannes moving by the Aalen road, Ney taking Lannes' place on the Stuttgart-Göppingen road.[2]

From the very commencement of the movement extreme friction developed between the Corps Commanders and the Chief of the Staff, adding immensely to the burden of correspondence borne by the Emperor. As an instance, the following case may be cited. Berthier had addressed to Murat certain orders mutually destructive of one another, and in reply the latter wrote (see vol. ii., p. 46):

> You have instructed me to occupy Göppingen on the 11th, Geislingen on the 12th, to send only a Division to Heidenheim on the 13th, and to remain with my headquarters at Göppingen, whilst in the last paragraph of your letter you express yourself as follows: 'The position of Heidenheim being very important for the enemy, it is necessary that Marshal Murat should hold it in force, and from the moment that he arrives he should send

2. This order was not issued to the Corps Commanders as a whole, but only by stages as it became evident to the Emperor that no movement by the enemy endangered its completion.

> news of all that he hears to the Marshals Soult and Davout, etc.' It is impossible in this circumstance to carry out the orders of his Majesty. I cannot remain at Göppingen when you order me to arrive in force at Heidenheim, and I cannot arrive in force at Heidenheim if you tell me to send only one Division to that place and to leave my Division of dismounted Dragoons to follow the Corps of Marshal Ney, Please, Monsieur le Marechal, explain yourself more clearly.

To this appeal Berthier only condescended to send the following reply:

> The Emperor has received your letter: he desires that you should follow your instructions and in consequence that you should carry out the prescribed movement.

But fortunately the Emperor gave no such instructions. On the contrary, knowing of the friction between the two subordinates, he himself wrote the following illuminating letter to Murat on the same date:

> You are to flank the whole of my march which is a delicate operation, as we are moving obliquely on the Danube. It is necessary therefore that if the enemy attempts to interfere, I should be warned in time to choose my own part and not be compelled to accept that which the enemy forces upon me. Hautpoul's Division must not follow your movement, it would only hamper your manoeuvring power. My intention is that it should follow my march, reaching Aalen at the same time that you attain Heidenheim. The dismounted Dragoons must be very tired; I shall keep them back till Marshal Ney has passed. I want them to be nursed. Marshal Ney will leave Stuttgart on the 4th October, and will follow you on Saturday the 5th. The dismounted Dragoons follow him, thus forming your reserve. Thus, on this

road, you will have 6000 Dragoons (mounted), Ney's Corps of 20,000 men and the dismounted Dragoons, in all 30 to 35,000 men. I shall be with the Corps of Marshal Lannes who passes by Gmünd; my Guards and d'Hautpoul's Division are a reserve to Lannes. You see, therefore, that if the enemy debouches from Ulm to attack my flank these two corps can be easily reinforced by a part of Soult's Corps.

In the last sentence there is evidently a hiatus, and the whole is evidently very hurriedly written or dictated, but the sense is clear and reveals the Emperor's intention exactly; but one is tempted to wonder what would have been the fate of the Grand Army without the astonishing gift of smoothing out difficulties which distinguished its Commander: would 30,000 additional men, even 60,000 have made up for his absence?

But it was not only Berthier's mistakes which threw additional work and worry on the Emperor's shoulders. From the very commencement of the march, the same jealousy and ill-feeling between his Marshals, which proved so fatal to the French arms in the Peninsula, began to manifest themselves. Thus Soult reports Davout to the Emperor for unpunctuality in following out the orders he had received, though the matter had nothing to do with Soult at all. He also complains that in passing he had taken up more than his share of biscuits from the magazines, which was probably true, but no more than Soult himself would have done had he only had the chance. Murat complains that Lannes did not move his troops out of Rastatt on his approach, and minor acts of interference in each others areas for requisition were frequent, nearly all of these requiring one of the soothing personal letters Napoleon knew so well how to write.

To provide for the contingency of an Austrian offensive on the left bank of the Danube, before the convergence of the road should have brought the columns within supporting distance, the chief command over the Bavarians, the 1st Corps and Marmont, was given to Bernadotte, the remainder—*viz*. Murat, Lannes, Ney, Soult, Davout and the Guard forming a single army under Napoleon's own direction as far, that is to say, as the indifferent nature of the cross-country roads communicating with the great highways on which the troops were marching would permit.

On the 3rd of October, the Grand Army reached the following positions: Bavarians at Forchheim, 1st Corps (Bernadotte) at Uffenheim, 2nd Corps (Marmont) from Rothenburg to Weikersheim both nearing Ansbach, the 3rd (Davout) and 4th (Soult) at Langenburg and Hall, the 5th (Lannes) and 6th (Ney) with the Cavalry (Murat) from Ludwigsburg to Füssen by Cannstadt, Stuttgart and Esslingen. The total front was about 120 miles, say six long days' marches over cross-country roads. The Bavarians were about 30 miles from Bernadotte, who was 14 miles from Marmont. Soult and Davout within 10 miles of each other Davout 16 miles from Marmont and 32 from Lannes—*i.e.* could only support him after a twenty four hours' forced march, assuming favourable conditions. All the Corps had orders to send representative Staff Officers to one another and to make all possible arrangements, by means of relays, inhabitants of the district, etc., to ensure rapid circulation of all information they might receive.

The Emperor had already begun to forecast his movements in case the Austrians attacked. If they issued from Donauwörth against Bernadotte, Soult and Davout were to march to his support, if from Ulm, Soult was to march to the assistance of the right wing, whilst Davout and Bernadotte continued their march towards the Danube.

Since the Emperor still believed the Austrians 20 per cent stronger than they really were, and Soult and Davout a long day's march from Bernadotte, Marmont, and the Bavarians, who hardly counted as combatants, with the country exceptionally favourable to the Austrian Cavalry, Bernadotte's prospects of a victory can hardly be described as satisfactory. Even the group on the right wing (supported by Soult, but only at the close of an exhausting march for the troops of the latter) would seem to an unprejudiced observer to have had but small chances of that absolute numerical superiority at the point of collision, which it was the whole end and object of Napoleon's subsequent strategical practice to bring about.

But in truth this idea of the absolute necessity of securing the maximum possible accumulation of force upon a particular fraction of the enemy's command seems as yet to have hardly occurred to his mind, for on the same day, with reference to a possible attack upon the centre of his line, he writes to Soult (vol. ii., p. 52):

> My intention is, that when we meet the enemy, we should envelop him on all sides.

But to envelop an enemy on all sides involves always the risk of being pulverised by his counterstroke at one point and with the weapons then in use, the numerical superiority on the whole theatre of war upon which he could count was quite inadequate as against the 88,000 men he still believed the Austrians could bring against him.

On the 4th October, Ney reached Füssen, Esslingen and Göppingen. Murat sent Beaumont to Weissenstein; Walther to Gingen, Altenstadt and Geislingen; Klein to Geislingen and towards Heidenheim. Lannes lay between Lorch and Waiblingen, followed by the Guard, Imperial headquarters, and d'Hautpoul's Cuirassiers.; Soult reached Bühlerthann and Gaildorf, 20 miles from Lannes and 18 from Ney; Davout was at Ilshofen, Marmont Rothenburg, Bernadotte Dachstetten and the Bavarians about Fürth.

So far no reliable information as to the enemy's movements had been obtained, they were known to be somewhere between the Danube, Iller and Lech, but whether they had concentrated about Ulm, Augsburg, Biberach or Memmingen remained entirely uncertain.

Whilst Murat was scouring the plains in vain endeavours to supply the prisoners[3] which the Emperor always so insistently demanded, and the remaining columns were closing up and by degrees assuming a more military formation, Bernadotte was encountering the critical incident of the whole campaign.

Nearing Ansbach, he found the gates of the little mediaeval fortress closed against him by its Prussian garrison. It was the Fort of Bard (1800) case over again, but with this distinction that, whether it held out two hours or a fortnight, a serious encounter would, we now know beyond any doubt, have brought a new and formidable opponent into the field. Fortunately for the French, the peculiar code of honour which had developed in the long-service armies of the Continent during the last century helped Bernadotte over the difficulty. War had become a matter of rules, like chess; and the letter of the code by which it was governed, not the spirit, sanctioned surrender to greatly superior forces to prevent the effusion of blood, and Bernadotte's persuasive tongue, backed by the exhibition of material force, soon proved sufficient to persuade the Prussian Commander to open his gates, thus setting in motion a stream of consequences which culminated a year later at the surrender of Prenzlau. Humanitarians would do well to follow up the whole chain of cause and effect and note the full total of suffering on the battlefield, and outside of it, which flowed from this single application of their favourite formula. It is not asserted that the defence of this little town could have averted the fall of Ulm under the circumstances which actually arose but the appearance of the Prussian Army on the scene would have inhibited Napoleon's further advance beyond Vienna, and it passes the wit of man to see how the Emperor could ever have fought his way back to France.

---

3. He only succeeded in capturing one.

In spite of Murat's activity (and he never spared himself), the Emperor was still dependent on his spies for information.

On the 2nd October they reported that works were being thrown up around Ulm and on the Iller. But as entrenchments had also been seen covering the exits from the Tyrol, no special conclusion could be gleaned from these facts; and on the 3rd a vague rumour announced the retreat of the Austrians towards the Lech. This also afforded nothing towards elucidating the situation.

On the 4th, however, more precise and significant reports arrived. The withdrawal of the enemy from Stokach, Biberach and Memmingen upon Ulm was confirmed, and Mack himself was said to have arrived at the latter place.

Donauwörth was unoccupied, but the arrival of the regiment "Colloredo" was expected, and six regiments of infantry with much cavalry had been seen moving from the west towards Lauingen.

On receipt of this information the Emperor at once ordered Murat to unite his three divisions of Dragoons at Heidenheim, whilst that of Bourcier moved on Geislingen, where it was to arrive on the 6th October and scout all the roads leading out of Ulm. In his covering letter he wrote:

> Bourcier's division of Dragoons is to cover the flank of the Army on the side of Geislingen. With your three divisions move on Heidenheim, in order to search out the whole plain towards Nordlingen. I assume that the enemy does not take up the offensive in which case you will act according to circumstances until further orders can reach you.
>
> Marshal Soult tells me that the enemy shows several squadrons between Nordlingen and Ellwangen. Whilst the Hussars of the 3rd Corps are skirmishing with them, it should be easy for you to cut them off from Donauwörth. I assume that the enemy has no considerable force

> at Nordlingen, only an advance guard to observe the plain in fact that *he still adheres to his plan of remaining behind the Danube.* If this is so, and he only has a couple of regiments of Infantry with as many Cavalry, try whether, with your 3000 Dragoons, you cannot cut them off in conjunction with the Light Cavalry of Lannes and Ney; if you warn Marshal Soult, all his Light Cavalry will come to join you. But do not attempt this if the enemy shows more than 6000 Infantry. What I want is information—send out agents, spies, and above all make some prisoners.

Meanwhile the Emperor began his preparations for the passage of the Danube, and ordered Soult to hasten the march of the pontoon trains, so that he could count on finding them there by the 6th or 7th October at latest.

> *Do not tell me that this is impossible,* requisition every horse for the purpose; mount the detachments in carriages and drive them night and day so that I may find at least five or six boats, if not the whole of them. On the river Wernitz, you will find timber boats under construction, and small rowing boats—try to surprise the lot, so that I may have means (in case the enemy has destroyed the arches of one or two permanent bridges) to capture it by a surprise crossing, and then restore it in a few hours. Get all the information you can and think this out. I need not tell you that I would prefer to cross the Danube between the Lech and Ingolstadt; nevertheless it will be very convenient for me to have means of passage about Donauwörth—partly to occupy the enemy; partly to assist the passage of my right.

To Davout also he wrote in the same strain; and though Marmont and Bernadotte were still far from the river, they too were ordered to lay hands on all boats and materials; and the conclusion of his letter to the latter deserves notice:

> One way or the other I want to cross the Danube at three points. Take the opinion of the Bavarian officers and let me have answers to the following questions:
> 1. Between Neuburg and Ingolstadt which is the most favourable point for crossing the Danube?
> 2. What means can you dispose of? Can you seize some boats on the Danube, or bring some with you from the little rivers in the neighbourhood?

Meanwhile, under cover of the screen thrown by Murat with his Cavalry, the remaining columns of the Army pursued their march with only trifling deviations from the original itinerary, though they suffered terribly from the exertions needed to keep their time, and stragglers were left behind with every mile.

By the morning of the 7th October they were all approaching the river, but since it would completely prejudice the mind of the reader against the conduct of the Austrian leaders to disclose at this point their exact location these details are held over until the drama, as it unrolled itself to Mack and his subordinates, has been sufficiently indicated.

Chapter 6

Austrian Operations: Passage of the Danube to the Battle of Elchingen

In the third chapter the movements of the Austrians were brought up to the 3rd October, on which day they occupied a position of readiness south of the Danube and east of the Iller, with small scouting detachments well away to their front. It would have been well had Mack left them there in peace to recuperate after their heavy marching but unfortunately his spies and scouts had by this time convinced him that the French were moving entirely on the left bank of the Danube, and that the appearance of troops in the defiles of the Black Forest, south of the Kinzig, were only feints to mislead him.

His front towards the Iller now seemed to him superfluous, and on the morning of the 4th October he ordered a closer concentration northward along the Danube from Ulm to Donauwörth, to be completed by the 8th. Simultaneously also, he drew up a new Order of Battle, with what precise intention it is now impossible to discover. To the modern student, especially on the Continent, who has generally grown up amongst divisions and Army Corps the composition of which has been unalterably fixed for generations, this tampering with the distribution of units in the field appears as a certain indication of aberration of intellect on the part of the Commander, and prejudices him against the latter's decisions throughout the campaign. But in the armies of those days such tampering was almost a matter of daily occurrence, and I only call attention again to it here to remind readers of what I have explained at length above, and to prevent their applying present-day principles to old-time customs for which there generally existed good and sufficient reasons. Probably Mack, knowing the atmosphere of distrust and jealousy by which he was surrounded, felt that it would be better to remove certain units from one command to the other to prevent seditious influences from spreading.

During the afternoon of the 6th October, Vandamme reached Harburg, and drove out the two squadrons of Liechtenstein Hussars placed there as an advance guard. These gave the alarm at Donauwörth, and the battalion of Colloredo, garrisoning the place, at once began to demolish the bridge over the Danube. But they were interrupted before their task was half finished, driven off by superior numbers, and by daylight Soult and Murat were streaming over the restored bridge in full pursuit.

Kienmayer, the Austrian General nearest at hand, fearing to be cut off from the main army, called in his detachments and began to retreat on Aichach, thence on Schwabhausen.

Mack rode out on 7th October to Günzburg, arriving there about 4 p.m. Here he was met by the news not only that the French had seized Donauwörth, but that Bernadotte had marched through Ansbach, and for the moment he thought of concentrating all available men and forcing his way through the French in order to rejoin Kienmayer, and with him to fall back towards the Inn.

The idea, however, seems to have been but momentary; it was impracticable into the bargain, for the troops were now engaged in moving into the new positions assigned to them by the order of the 4th October. Also, as the weather had broken up altogether during the preceding forty-eight hours, it was impossible to locate the many detachments exactly, or to calculate how long any orders might take in reaching them.

Against the principle of this move there is nothing to be said; but as events turned out it would have been better to have had the men thoroughly rested in their cantonments of the 3rd than worn out, weary and widely dispersed, in point of time, on the wretched cross-country tracks they were actually following.

By next morning (8th October) this first thought had evidently been dismissed because Mack wrote to Kutusov in the following terms:

> We have enough to live upon in the district west of the Lech—more than enough in fact to last us until the Russian Army reaches the Inn, and will be ready to move. Then we shall easily find the opportunity to prepare for the enemy the fate he deserves.

This letter is of particular importance because it establishes a strong *prima facie* case for the genuineness of Mack's pamphlet prepared after the events in justification of his conduct. It proves at least that he had an idea of the strength of his position, and was determined to make the most of it.[1] As this pamphlet contains the only complete account of the working of Mack's mind, I give the following passages almost verbatim:

> When on the 7th October we learnt of the march of Bernadotte and the Bavarians through Ansbach, it would no longer have been possible to withdraw the Army behind (i.e. to the eastward of) the Lech, as it was then on the march towards the Danube, moving in many small columns. . . . This led me to decide for the concentration on Günzburg, to secure communication with Kienmayer, who was still east of the Lech, and with him to fall on

1. See *Mémoires justificatifs*, p. 9 *et seq.* I quote from the French *Official History*, as no copy of the original can be traced in England.

the heads of the enemy's columns as opportunity offered either east or west of the Lech. But in saying that it was too late to order the retirement behind the Lech, I do not mean to imply that I would have given the order had it been possible. I would not have done so at any time, even had I been able to foresee the violation of Prussian territory; indeed this very violation in itself made it my duty not to withdraw the army. . . .

To withdraw the army behind the Inn, to sacrifice Tyrol, the Vorarlberg and the Army of Italy, was a resolution only permissible to the supreme power of his Majesty. The enemy would have overtaken us in superior numbers, and we should have been thrown back upon the Russian columns. . . .

It would have been still worse to retire beyond the Inn to leave the valleys of Salzburg and Upper Austria unoccupied. . . . The battle of Austerlitz would then have taken place before Vienna—and who can tell with what far-reaching results.

" The situation of the Army was certainly gravely compromised by the sudden appearance of an enemy more than twice its superior in numbers, but I did not consider it desperate. At the moment that I became certain that he had occupied both banks of the Lech at the bridge of Rain; that he had compelled the Corps of Kienmayer to retreat and that he could reach Augsburg before we could finally when his project to cut us off from the Russians became clearly manifest from that moment I decided to fall in turn upon his communications, break his superiority, and draw him away from the Russians. It was still open to us to retreat into Tyrol, but I rejected the alternative because it would have meant sacrificing our Allies, since the French would have reached them by the shortest line, long before we could accomplish the long detour through the valleys of Tyrol and Salzburg.

I believe rather that I deserve praise for my resolution, suddenly taken, for our communications would have remained open,[2] and we should have had at our disposal behind us Bohemia, Franconia and Saxony for eventual retreat and subsistence.

We could live by requisitions as well as the enemy, and had a right to expect that we should be well received by the Prussians of Ansbach and by the Saxons; probably the disposition of Prussia towards us (then so amicable as a consequence of the storm of rage evoked by the violation of her territories) would never have taken the unfavourable turn it has since undergone.

These motives would have prevented my retreat behind the Inn even had I been able to foresee the violation of Prussian neutrality; for is it possible to imagine a situation more encouraging, from the military point of view for Prussia, than to have an Austrian Army covering her frontiers and those of Saxony, whilst both countries were mobilising and ready to unite with their forces against the common enemy? I affirm that up to the moment when our concentration on Günzburg was rendered impossible, and our existence on the left, and in Ulm, annihilated, I considered this violation of neutrality as a good fortune, in spite of the confusion into which it plunged us, and I have received two letters, one from Count Cobenzl, the other from Count Lamberti, proving clearly that his Majesty was with them in the same opinion.

We were provided with sufficient artillery and ammunition for some time, certainly for three battles, for we had with us all our reserves of artillery, both heavy and light, and could always have drawn something from Bohemia, as a glance at the map suffices to show. The reinforce-

2. *Car nos communications s'en trouvaient dégages*, in the original.

ments still on the march were indeed lost to my army, but not to the common cause, as they could join our Allies on the Inn whilst those coming from Italy could guard the passes of Tyrol and would indeed be of more use to us there, because a force of from 35,000 to 40,000 men was best for my purpose and this is about what remained after the departure of Jellacic for the Vorarlberg, and of Kienmayer, destined to join the Russians.

The enemy was thus placed between two adversaries and obliged to divide himself into two Armies, for he was far more dependent on his communications than were we, having with him but the bare minimum of artillery and ammunition. . . . Whilst we, if we were beaten, could retire in any direction except the Rhine; and our project of drawing off the bulk of the enemy, and thus gaining time for the arrival of the Russians, would have been completely attained.

If he employed against us forces notably superior to ours, we could always give way before him, because except towards the Rhine we were free to retreat in any direction, and the further we went the more completely should we obtain the chief purpose of our design *viz.* to keep the bulk of the enemy's forces away from the Allied Armies. . . . There cannot be a doubt that quite different results would have followed the adoption of this plan; if they had not been altogether satisfactory, at least they would have been less disastrous than those which actually befell us.

On the 8th October, whilst Mack was drawing up fresh dispositions, Aufenberg arrived at Wertingen. It was then about 7 a.m. Here orders reached him, cancelling his instructions to march towards the Lech, and directing him to return to Zumarshausen to cover the road to Augsburg, and constituting his command the advance guard of the whole army.

At the same time he learnt that French troops marching

towards him had passed through the village of Nordendorf—*i.e.* were close at hand. Notwithstanding his orders and this information, he resolved to canton his troops at Wertingen.

The gates of the little place were defended by three battalions of infantry. The Grenadiers took their rest in the streets and the cavalry found what quarters they could outside the walls.

About noon, news was brought to Aufenberg that some French troops had passed through Pfaffenhofen about 4½ miles away and he resolved to attack them in the hope of disclosing the position of the main force.

To this end, he formed a detachment, under the orders of General Dinersberg, consisting of 2 squadrons of Cuirassiers, 2 companies of Grenadiers, and 2 companies of Fusiliers, and Dinersberg in his turn divided this command into two equal halves, sending one by the right bank of the Zusam on Thiersheim, the other by the left bank on Frauenstetten. Probably their commanders divided their detachments in the same manner, and so on. Be this as it may, the reconnaissance found the French near both villages, was at once overwhelmed by superior numbers, and driven back in considerable disorder to Wertingen.

As soon as the first fugitives arrived with tidings of misfortune, Aufenberg drew up four battalions of Grenadiers on the heights to the left of the road to Günzburg; one before the gate of Augsburg, and another with two additional companies were detailed to hold the Pfaffenhofen gate. The remaining three battalions occupied the town itself, and the two and a half squadrons available were formed up in support of the right wing of the four battalions to the left of the Günzburg road.

These dispositions had hardly been completed when news arrived that two whole French corps were approaching, one on either bank of the Zusam. A French cavalry regiment drove in the Grenadiers before the Augsburg gate, and then fell upon the Cuirassiers stationed upon the heights, but this attack was checked by the fire of the Infantry behind them.

Aufenberg, seeing his position untenable, now decided to retreat on Günzburg, but his orders could no longer be carried out. The French everywhere outnumbered and overlapped his positions. The troops engaged in the defence of Wertingen were surrounded and cut off, the General himself was taken prisoner, and ultimately only 2 guns and some 1400 Grenadiers reached Zumarshausen, where for the time being they found safety.

Comment: Altogether this little action caused the Austrians, according to their own accounts, a loss of 101 killed and 233 wounded; 1469 prisoners, 3 colours and 6 guns; about 1000 more men were missed, but these rejoined their colours after a time. I have dwelt upon it at some length because it shows so strikingly the difference between the tactical tendencies of the two armies. Had the roles been reversed, the French General having made up his mind that it was his duty to obtain information would have moved off with his whole command in hand, and attacked to hold, thus forcing the enemy to disclose his dispositions, and leaving them open to the attack of any other French troops in the vicinity, who, in accordance with the traditions of the Republican Armies not yet broken down by Napoleon, would have marched at once to the sound of the guns. The Austrians, thinking only of *seeing*, not of *compelling*, divided and subdivided their commands, *thus frittering away their striking force*, and when they found the French at last, it was the old story over again of the man who caught the Tartar.

Early on the morning of the 9th, Mack, who was just about to commence his march from Günzburg to Zumarshausen, received the intelligence of his subordinate's misfortune, and being perfectly certain of encountering very superior forces if he proceeded on his way, at once ordered his columns to stand fast.

His counsellors strongly urged upon him the necessity of retreating by Memmingen to Tyrol. But Mack had no intention of being guilty of any such pusillanimous conduct. Instead of that he decided to cross over the Danube, take up a position between Giengen and Heidenheim and attack the French troops still on the left bank of the river, thus threatening Napoleon's communications, and compelling him to desist from his march towards the Inn.

In support of this operation Jellacic was sent back to Memmingen to make demonstrations towards the Lech. A flying column was to be sent from Ulm towards Geislingen to attack the French convoys about Stuttgart. The Corps of Klenau, Gottesheim and Werneck were to follow one another at intervals of three hours along the road from Ulm to Albeck during the 11th and the ensuing night. Ulm itself was to be abandoned, as it was impossible to complete its armament, and no troops could be spared as a garrison.

These were Mack's ideas, when the French suddenly attacked the detachment under d'Aspre, who had been sent on to the left bank of the river to protect the bridge which then crossed it at Günzburg. D'Aspre had "hugged" his charge too closely, and when the French came on with their usual rapidity his force was cut in half, the bridge seized and he himself taken prisoner, before his flanks had time to make good their retreat.

Fortunately a battalion in Günzburg itself made a sturdy resistance, and before this could be overcome, the main body of Mack's command coming from Burgau appeared on the scene and deployed on the heights overlooking the town and the river—the right at Liepach, the left at Reissenburg—and holding all the bridges as far as Leipheim.

During the fight the bridge over the Danube had been broken up, but in the evening orders were given to the Austrians to repair it. The French did not interfere with their working parties, but as soon as the work was completed, a heavy fire was poured in upon the defenders and the French troops captured it with a rush, establishing themselves securely in some small copses on either side of the road.

The losses to the Austrians for that day were about 800 killed and wounded, with about 1000 prisoners.

The direct road to the left bank being thus closed against the Austrians, the Archduke Ferdinand, who had arrived during the course of the action, proposed to Mack either to march at once to the bridge of Elchingen or retreat on Tyrol.

Fortunately—for the Elchingen bridge was also seized by the French a few hours later during the night—Mack fell in with neither suggestion, but decided to withdraw to Ulm.

But this disappointment hit Mack very hard, as the following extract from his *Justification* will show:

> I must repeat that this event was all the more unexpected because the detachment sent to observe beyond the Danube under General d'Aspre had not sent us the least warning of the enemy's approach. The Army having encamped with its left on the Danube close to the bridge, and having been attacked seven or eight hours later in the afternoon, it can hardly be said that there was not sufficient connection with the observing detachment and an adequate possibility of supporting it at once.
>
> At the moment I was busy drawing up the orders for the passage across the river by night, with all the details that this operation involved. *This order took up eight pages, in the whole of which it would be difficult to find a superfluous word*, and it will be easily understood that all my attention and thoughts were absorbed by such a work. Moreover the minor details of the service of security formed no part of my duties, but should have been attended to by the detachment commanders themselves, or better still, by the premier Aide-de-Camp General. It is not his duty to draw up projects, but to ensure the execution of those prepared by the Quartermaster-General which have been approved by the Commander-in-Chief.

During the night of the 10th October the main body of the Austrian Army marched back to Ulm and went into camp on either side of the river.

Comment: To judge by the diary of an Austrian Staff Officer, on which the authors of the French *Official History* place their chief reliance for information concerning the state and spirit of the troops, but which being written after the event seems to me to need much correction to allow for the "personal equation," the troops were broken and dispirited, mere shadows of their former selves. This constant marching in the awful weather, which had already lasted nearly a fortnight, and the want of most of the creature comforts to which the Austrians had always been accustomed (one of the consequences of the attempt to introduce the French system of requisition) had affected all ranks alike, and the senior officers openly expressed their doubts and anxieties.

Probably in the hopes of checking the effect on the men of this growing spirit of insubordination, Mack chose this very inopportune moment to redistribute the regiments amongst the several commands. It is inconceivable that a man of Mack's experience would have taken such a step, even granted that in the old long service organisations it was not nearly so unusual or serious a step as at the present day, unless it had been forced upon him by overwhelming necessity. It seems to me that nothing gives us a better scale for judging the difficulties by which he was surrounded than the fact that he was compelled to have recourse to it.

Probably this measure was hastened by the severe differences of opinion which on this very night broke out between the Archduke and Mack. During the course of the evening the former received a letter[3] from the Emperor couched in the following words:

---

3. *Campagne d'Allemagne.* Vol. III., p. 173.

My Cousin,

The orders I am sending you today will show how seriously I view the situation.

When I was at Landsberg, you put forward the desire (expressed with commendable modesty) to receive from me an instruction which would settle completely your line of conduct in the case of differences of opinion arising between you and General Mack, as to the operations of the army entrusted to you. I promised at the time to think over the matter; but now when you may be called upon to take resolutions on which the safety of the Empire may depend, and which can only be determined on the spot itself, I consider that I shall be rendering a true service to you by inviting you to follow the advice of F.M.L. Mack who has already rendered such great services to me and possesses such wide experience.

Francois

The contents of this letter, as in duty bound, the Archduke communicated to Lieut. Field-Marshal Mack. There seems to be no record of what actually passed between them but in the end the Archduke formally declared that, having been deprived of all initiative, he refused henceforward to accept any responsibility.

What Mack thought of the matter may be deduced from the following report of a conversation, between him and F.M.L. Gyulai, which took place in the presence of Col. Bianchi, his A.D.C. This is quoted by the authors of the *Campagne d'Allemagne* in a note, but with no specific reference as to its source:

His Royal Highness cannot really imagine that he is charged with the command of an army. He is far too young and inexperienced to fill such a role. His Majesty has conferred on me full powers for these operations and I am responsible to him in the fullest degree.

He then went on to assert that the Archduke had been

perfectly aware of the Emperor's instructions on this point ever since the interview at Landsberg, and suggested that he had kept back the Emperor's letter (which it will be noted is undated) until the present difficult situation had arisen.

The Archduke acknowledged the receipt of the Emperor's letter in a script too long for reproduction. The spirit of it was however exactly what one would have expected from a young and inexperienced officer, who saw the sufferings and troubles all around him, but had not experience enough to trace them back to their proper source and lay the blame on the right shoulders.

In reading it, one is irresistibly reminded of the similar screeds poured out by columns from the fluent pens of our modern war correspondents in South Africa.

Mack himself in his justification asserts specifically that, in this interview on the night of the 10th October, the Archduke refused to allow him to read the letter with his own eyes; and this statement, if accepted, is enough to put the Archduke out of court altogether. Unfortunately, at this point the narrative of the *Campagne d'Allemagne* loses its customary clearness, and discloses a bias in favour of the young Prince. This is altogether unaccountable in officers of a Republican Army, whose sympathies one would naturally have expected to find on the side of the experienced "ranker" instead of with an inexperienced scion of the aristocracy, and I must leave it to the context to reveal to which side the weight of the whole evidence inclines.

On the morning of the 11th October Mack submitted the following draft of his proposed reorganisation of the Army for the Archduke's *visa*:

> 1. The Army to be formed at once in three Corps, each of which is to have its due proportion of light troops, line, and reserve—*i.e.* light troops one quarter, line or main body one half, Reserve Corps, one quarter.[4]

4. The reader's attention is particularly called to the extraordinary vagueness with which the term "corps" is here applied. Compare it with my remarks on this subject in *The Leipzig Campaign* (Leonaur, 2007).

Each Corps Commander to detail permanently from his advance guard, two battalions with two 3-pdr. guns and two light squadrons well mounted, under the orders of a picked officer, ready to be employed at a moment's notice either as vanguard, flanking party or flying column. Each will also detail for his special service, a selected Captain of Cavalry with 4 N.C.O.'s and 40 troopers.

Note. The Corps of Jellacic should have besides at least six or eight squadrons.

2. These orders to be communicated at once to the Corps Commanders for immediate action.

3. All important reports received by your Royal Highness to be sent on to me, so that I can add my opinion in a few words. Instructions or orders sent out from your R. Highness's headquarters to be sent to me first for countersignature.

Comment: The two remaining paragraphs are omitted as unimportant; the above are sufficient to reveal the possibilities of friction and disaster between the two men, and the loss of time bound to ensue unless the two staffs habitually rode together—but this was by no means their practice.

During the course of the morning the Army took up a position on the heights to the north of Ulm—only one brigade of Schwarzenberg's command remaining on the right bank of the Danube. About noon, guns were heard from the direction of Albeck, and a column of French Infantry was seen issuing from the woods and entering into Jüngingen. This, as we shall see hereafter, was part of Dupont's detachment operating entirely unsupported by the rest of the French Army.

The nearest troops at hand under Loudon at once moved against them and, after a pretty sharp tussle, drove them out of the village. Meanwhile Schwarzenberg and Klenau, placing themselves at the head of the Cuirassier Regiments "Mack" and "Archduke Charles," to which some other squadrons rallied, making 18 squadrons in all, threw themselves upon the French right and rear, riding over and almost destroying 2 regiments of cavalry and one of infantry, and bringing in 2 eagles, 11 guns and some 800 to 900 prisoners..

Mack himself was wounded in this skirmish, and one is tempted to ask *"que diable allait-il faire dans cette galere?"* It surely formed no part of his duty, whether as Chief of Staff or Commander in Chief, to allow himself to be involved in a quite unimportant affair of outposts.

Over and above the eagles, guns and prisoners, the orders to the 6th Corps (Ney) were captured, instructing it to attack and carry Ulm from the left bank, whilst the rest of the Army moved up against it from the south. This piece of information was of extreme importance, as it showed that the road to Bohemia was still open, but unfortunately circumstances combined to prevent immediate action from being taken.

Mack's own account in his *Justification* sheds some light on what these circumstances were, and reveals again the impossibility of the situation created by the insubordination of the Archduke:

> When the news of the enemy's attack arrived, his Imperial Highness at once rode out of Ulm with several Generals and their A.D.C.'s without giving me time to join them, or leaving word where I might find them. For myself, I went as soon as possible to Michelsberg, the key of our position, expecting to find his Imperial Highness there. I was disappointed, but learnt that he was in an entrenchment on our right. Events compelled me to remain where I was for the five hours during which the engagement lasted, separated from him by a distance of a couple of miles, whence resulted the fact that the enemy was only beaten on his right by our left, whereas he should have been enveloped and annihilated had his Imperial Highness been with me on our left,

> for I should have begged him to have sent the necessary orders to ensure this result. But nothing of the kind was possible. Our right remained inert, because it was not my place to send orders to his Imperial Highness, with whom was Feldzeugmeister Kollowrath, and I had reason to hope that the latter or some of the other Generals, or the Adjutant General, with him, would have given him the necessary advice to attack.

Mack desired to profit at once by the advantages his troops had undoubtedly gained in this combat of Haslach, and the important improvement in the morale of the men which undoubtedly had resulted from it. His idea was to march out by the left bank of the river towards Ratisbon, to reach a hand to the Russians whom he had reason to believe to be in the vicinity. But Werneck and others represented the fatigue of the men as so extreme that his project had to be abandoned for the day. In his *Justification* he protests against this view as follows:

> How is it possible to put forward this plea of exhaustion as a reason for delaying our departure until the 13th, when it is notorious that all the troops, including Werneck's command, had reposed peacefully during the night of the 11th after the fight, and had all the day of the 12th to recover from the disorganisation which the fight had entailed? F.M.L. Werneck opposed my proposition with altogether improper violence before the Prince, and his Imperial Highness tolerated his protests, although I went so far as to request that his Imperial Highness would allow me to start with Werneck's Corps so that I could prove that my proposal contained no impossibility either for himself or for his men.
>
> The Prince, however, would not accede to my request, although he had thrown the whole responsibility on my shoulders only two days before, and had in his possession the Imperial Order to decide in my favour when

> I insisted upon my point. I only requested his Imperial Highness to call the principal Generals together in order to explain to them verbally my plans. I had no intention of consulting with them at all.

The 12th, therefore, was spent as a day of rest, but when in the evening news came in of the retreat of the French behind the Brenz, whilst 20,000 to 30,000 were reported advancing on the right bank towards Weissenhorn, Mack recurred to his original purpose with slight modifications. His *Justification* continues:

> When the news of the appearance of several columns of the enemy moving on the Iller reached me, I acquired the conviction that the main body of the enemy was turning towards us, wishing at all costs to secure the possession of Ulm. It became necessary therefore to leave some 12,000 to 13,000 men in that town—*i.e.* the Corps of Schwarzenberg.
>
> My first project, drafted during the morning of the 12th, had been to send Werneck's Corps on Geislingen, to reach that place on the 13th and to detach columns towards Stuttgart, possibly even to the Rhine; whilst on the morning of the 13th the two Corps of Riesch and Schwarzenberg were to attack the Corps of Ney and pass *beyond the Danube or along the river.*[5] My second project was, since Ney's Corps had taken position at Langenau and, it was alleged, had received reinforcements, to attack it on the morning of the 13th. To these two projects I added, that after the enemy on the left bank had been driven off, the Reserve Artillery and Convoys should file out of Ulm towards Heidenheim and further

5. I underline these words to direct attention to the extraordinary confusion of Mack's narrative, which may perhaps be accounted for by the state of his mind when these words were written. The same remark may be reasonably applied throughout his writings.

if necessary; whilst the Corps of Jellacic occupied Ulm and acted on the right bank against the enemy should he approach from Gunzburg. We still believed the chief efforts of the French to be directed eastwards against the Russians and imagined we had only a detachment of observation to deal with.

When, however, the news of the approach of a strong body of the enemy marching towards the Iller arrived, a third disposition became necessary, and Jellacic was sent along the left bank of the Iller in order to withdraw towards the Tyrol if necessary; whilst the news simultaneously received of Ney's retreat beyond the Danube allowed us to send off the Reserve Artillery and the Convoys to Heidenheim immediately. Indeed we were driven to this resolution by the apparent desire of the enemy to cross the Danube above Ulm, which would have compromised their ulterior departure.

For their security the Corps of Riesch was detailed to watch the left bank of the Danube *as far as Heidenheim*, and Werneck was ordered to Heidenheim.

Hence of the four 'Corps d'Armée' that of Schwarzenberg alone remained at Ulm, or rather beyond Ulm on the right bank. It was ordered to reconnoitre on the 13th the enemy's column seen near Weissenhorn overnight, and on the 14th to leave Richter's brigade at Ulm as garrison, and to follow with the remainder to Albeck on the road to Heidenheim.

In the meantime, thanks to Werneck's opposition, the troops were suffering considerably more from the hunger entailed by their continued presence in and around Ulm than they would have done in marching over a fresh area, and the spirits of the men drooped hourly as they waited under streaming rain in the muddy bivouacs. But at length, early on the morning of the 13th, they moved off. Werneck was on the left, taking with him all the Reserve Artillery, the pontoons and heavy trains—Riesch in the centre, along the Danube towards Elchingen and Langenau, and the right under Schwarzenberg on the right bank of the river towards Weissenhorn to observe the movements of the enemy on the right bank of the Danube, and to delay his movements until dark, then to retreat on Ulm, march through the town and follow Riesch on the 14th to Langenau. Jellacic also was despatched up the left bank of the Iller to remove boats and destroy the bridges, ultimately to make good his retreat towards the Lake of Constance and Tyrol. Only 5 to 6 battalions with 4 squadrons were to be left behind as garrison for Ulm.

As usual, the "order of battle" of the several commands had been again readjusted, and as the columns marched off Werneck disposed of three Divisions, totalling 25 battalions and 3 rifle companies, together with 16 squadrons but all greatly reduced in numbers; one battalion, for instance, which had suffered very severely at Wertingen mustered only 200 bayonets. Riesch broke up his 32 battalions and 12 squadrons into two columns, of approximately equal strength; the first under Loudon moved between the main road to Heidenheim and the Danube by. cross country tracks leading to Gundelfingen; the latter under Riesch himself by Thalfingen—*i.e.* following the river bank towards Elchingen. But by this time the roads were so broken up by the continuous rain that in places they were almost impassable, and the six to seven miles from Ulm to Elchingen took fourteen hours, while wagons without number remained behind hopelessly stuck in the mud. Nevertheless, the Advance Guards ultimately reached Elchingen and drove out the French outposts, seized the bridge, removed some of the planking, and having prepared it for demolition, settled down for the night believing themselves perfectly secure against attack from that quarter at least. The rest of the troops seem to have slept in the mud just where darkness overtook them, for daylight found them still scattered about the country unable to concentrate against a sudden attack.

Werneck, on higher ground and better roads, was between Heidenheim and Herbrechtingen, and as far as he was concerned the road lay practically open to him.

Meanwhile Mack, in Ulm, was receiving constant reports of the approach of larger bodies of French troops on the roads coming from Leipheim, Weissenhorn and Pfaffendorf. Deserters and prisoners declared that the whole army was behind them, and the Austrian outposts were slowly driven back towards the Iller. Finally, he learnt that the whole of Ney's Corps, last heard of on the left bank of the Danube, had crossed over to the right bank.[6]

This intelligence completely mystified him; and now there occurred one of those extraordinary chances of war, which sometimes arise to mislead even the soundest of intellects. About 10 a.m., a report reached him, founded on a conversation overheard at a *table d'hote* in a village between Stuttgart and Ulm, that the British had effected a landing at Boulogne, and that a revolution had broken out somewhere in France. The man who brought the news merely repeated what he had heard for what it was worth, but the idea seems to have appealed to Mack's imagination, and this is what he deduced from the information now before him:

> If the enemy wished to secure Ulm, the right bank was certainly not the side from which to approach it, since the town itself lies entirely on the left bank. If he meant to invest it, then he required to be in at least equal strength on both banks but he had withdrawn practically all his strength from the left bank of the river and was approaching by several roads on the south side.

6. This, it will be seen, in the account of the French movements, was premature by several hours.

> This gave me the impression of a retreat, rather than of an advance; for an Army on the Lech wishing to retire on the Rhine and knowing Ulm to be held by an enemy would have acted in no other manner. The news brought me by Baron Steinherr, a credible witness, of the conversation he had overheard, coincided so well with the opinions I had already formed on the facts before me, that I allowed myself to accept it as correct, all the more so because no more favourable moment for a British landing, and a revolutionary outbreak could well be imagined than this one, when Bonaparte at the head of all his mobilised resources was away beyond the Rhine. It was further rumoured that Prussia, exasperated by the violation of her neutrality, was on the point of declaring War against him. . . .

Buoyed up by this new hope, Mack prepared a general order announcing to the troops still lying around Ulm that the French were in full retreat towards the Rhine in three columns; and ordering each command to detail two flying columns, to pursue and harass the retreating enemy. We may pass over the details, since events moved faster than the orders themselves travelled, and the Austrian Commanders found quite other tasks to their hands to be dealt with.

For a moment, on the receipt of this information, as Mack afterwards confessed, his first idea had been to attack the French with all his forces on the right bank in the direction of Weissenhorn but the vision of a pursuit of the retreating enemy was too fascinating to be foregone, and in an unlucky moment, like the fox in the fable he threw away the substance for the shadow.[7]

---

7. In defence of the ready acceptance by Mack of the rumour of a British landing at Boulogne and all the consequences that would follow such an occurrence, it must be pointed out that Mack knew that the Austrian Government had made most pressing representations to the Cabinet of St James as to the desirability of this diversion, and the British Government were in fact preparing forces for such a descent all through the autumn.

Comment: I write this advisedly, for an attack at this moment would have "held" the enemy. Their columns converging inwards from all sides would doubtless have annihilated Schwarzenberg's command but Ney's march towards Elchingen would have been arrested, and since the Austrians on the left bank, in consequence of the mud, could not have retraced their steps in time to intervene, their retreat to the north-eastward would still have remained open, and beyond the reach of French molestation.

14th October. During the night of the 13th-14th October, the Austrians on the left bank of the Danube rested in complete security. They knew that Dupont's Division had retired to the Brenz—and having prepared the bridge at Elchingen for demolition and arranged to seize the bridges down stream at Riedheim, Leipheim, and Gundelfingen at early dawn, there remained no cause for further anxiety.

Unfortunately for them the French, having at last straightened out the series of Staff blunders which had led to the transfer of their whole army (less Dupont) to the right bank, were marching with all haste to undo the consequences of their previous mistakes, and in the morning detachments of their troops entered Riedheim and Leipheim immediately before the Austrians came up. A few moments later Ney himself arrived at the bridge of Elchingen; and his leading detachments attacked with suddenness and impetuosity, individuals swarming over the road-bearers of the bridge with such daring and rapidity that the contemplated demolition of the structure had to be abandoned, and presently the village from which the bridge takes its name, together with the copses and meadows lying between the village and the river, was in French hands whilst flanking columns were hastening up from Riedheim and Leipheim farther down stream.

Seeing that the line of the Danube had fallen, Riesch drew

up the troops immediately at hand along the track from Ober Elchingen to Oetingen, and summoned Loudon and all the men within his call to his aid.

But they had straggled terribly during the previous days' march, and the roads were still almost impassable. Hence the French, pouring over the river at the several crossing places, penetrated between the converging columns and began attacking them in flank. The surprise in fact proved altogether too complete for the Austrians, and though their closed detachments fought most gallantly, and their cavalry, in spite of their exhausted horses and diminished effectives, charged by squadrons again and again, their plucky resistance soon broke down, and a general retreat began. The troops fell back in the usual manner, by the tracks by which they had come—*i.e.* towards Ulm, leaving behind them about 4000 killed, wounded and prisoners—*i.e.* about 30 per cent, of their strength.

Nearing Ulm, Riesch found Schwarzenberg occupying the Michelsberg and Geisberg on the left of the Danube with his Corps, and by degrees his shattered command formed up behind this still intact screen.

As Werneck, who was still pursuing his march along the Heidenheim Road, had with him all the Reserve Artillery, no heavy guns were left to strengthen the position, a fact which had an important influence on subsequent events.

Jellacic's detachment marching in execution of its orders, south on Memmingen, and well served by its light troops, on learning that this town had capitulated to Soult and was now held by French troops in force, bent off eastward to Wangen and, passing thus behind the French columns, made good his retreat to Tyrol.

CHAPTER 7

French Movements from the 6th October to the Battle of Elchingen

7th October. On the night of the 6th October Soult and Murat lay a short distance from Donauwörth, which had been seized by the advance guard of Vandamme's Division (Soult's Corps) about 8 p.m. but the Austrians in retreating had had time to cut the bridge behind them. Immediately Soult and Murat made their dispositions to pass the river both above and below it, and the enemy having no men available to guard these passages, retreated next morning about 10 a.m. the 7th October. The bridge was at once repaired, and the French streamed over in hot pursuit. Again the Austrians endeavoured to make a stand and destroyed the bridge at Rain, on the Lech, but the French dragoons, passing some miles below the town, threatened their line of retreat and again compelled a withdrawal.

The Emperor himself arrived at Donauwörth during the morning, and with the passage of the river thus in his hands, immediately decided to direct Ney against Ulm by both banks of the river, securing all the bridges on his way. Ney should have halted this day at Giengen, but apparently the order never reached him, for, in fact, he arrived at Hochstaedt during the evening, and bivouacked in and around that place, leaving Dupont's Division at Diesenhofen.

Of Soult's Corps (IV.) Vandamme's Division bivouacked near Rain. Legrand and Saint Hilaire only reached Donauwörth, ready to cross early next morning; Suchet's Division and the Imperial Guard lay along the road from Nordlingen to Donauwörth, where the Emperor took up his quarters. The V. Corps reached the bridge of Minister, and the Cavalry Divisions of Bourcier and Baraguey-d'Hilliers lay about Neresheim, their scouts watching the roads leading out of Ulm.

Davout, marching on Neuburg, reached Monheim; Marmont was at Pappenheim; Bernadotte and the Bavarians at Weissenburg, with his advance guards at the gates of Ingolstadt.

The events of the 7th, however, brought no fresh intelligence to the Emperor. He knew that the Austrians had been concentrating around Ulm, which they were to reach on the 6th, but he had only a vague idea of what troops Mack actually had with him about the Iller. Further, he was unable to predict whether Mack, on learning of the appearance of the French at Rain, would remain where he was or attempt to escape envelopment by a rapid march by either of the roads leading to Landsberg or Augsburg.

The working of his mind is best shown by the following letter which he caused to be sent to Ney during the night of the 7th-8th October:

> It is probable that the passage of the Lech (at Rain) and the occupation of Augsburg, which will take place during the course of the day, will open the enemy's eyes.... It is impossible, when he hears of the passage of the Danube and the Lech, *together with the terror which must have seized upon his troops*,[1] which he had beyond the Lech, that he can fail to think seriously of retreat. It is to be expected

1. I have italicised the words, "with the terror," etc., because neither the Austrian nor the French narratives of the troops actually engaged on the 7th disclose anything approaching panic on the Austrian side. In fact, at the close of the day, the cavalry of the latter turned on their pursuers with considerable vigour and effect.

> that he will first try the road to Augsburg, but learning as he soon will that it is too late, he will then try Landsberg where if our troops arrive in time he will stand to fight, or perhaps continue to retreat on Tyrol. More probably he will decide to fight.
>
> His Majesty does not think that the enemy can be mad enough to cross to the left bank of the Danube, as his magazines are all at Memmingen, and he has the greatest possible interest not to separate himself from Tyrol.

Later on he wrote personally to Ney:

> I cannot believe that the enemy can have any other plan but to retreat on Augsburg or Landsberg, or even on Füssen. Anyhow he may hesitate, and in that case it lies with us to arrange that not one escapes.

With this idea in his mind he calculated that it might come to a battle on the 9th, on the Lech. Accordingly he sent orders to the 2nd, 3rd, 4th, and 5th Corps to hasten their march so as to have sufficient men in hand about Augsburg on the 9th.

Comment: We do not know at what hour these orders were sent out, still less at what time they actually reached the troops. The fact, however, is that they were physically beyond their powers to execute; for only Vandamme's Division lay south of the Danube, and the others mentioned had none of them less than 26 miles to march, while Marmont and Davout were nearly 40 miles away from their destination. In fine weather such a march would have been phenomenal even for the Grand Army, and with the roads in the terrible state they are known to have presented, one may frankly put such a feat down as impossible. On the other hand, assuming the Austrians to have completed their concentration on the 6th October (as apparently Napoleon believed that they had done) and given the better road over which they had to pass, they ought to have reached Augsburg with about 70,000 men (including Kienmayer already in the vicinity) before Soult with his 30,000 who could only be supported by driblets from hour to hour. Ultimately of course the victory of five French Corps over two Austrian ones was assured, and no doubt Mack was well advised not to make the attempt, but with the rapid decision still possible in those days for an army strong in Cavalry and trained to attack in "line" it is quite within the limits of probability that the Austrians should have destroyed Soult and then, deflecting their march on Landsberg, have made good their retreat into Tyrol. This, however, though it would have saved Mack's reputation, would not have gained time for the union of the Russians and Austrians on the Inn which it was the whole purpose of Mack's mission to obtain.[2]

Actually, the troops were far from having attained the destinations assigned to them in previous orders for the 8th October. Several delays in the march and in the delivery of orders kept back Ney's Corps till late at night. The columns of Marmont and Bernadotte crossed each other on the march, and neither of them reached their destinations on the Danube by several miles. Davout bivouacked with his main body at Neuburg, his advance guard being some six miles farther south on the way to Aichach.

Soult's Corps fouled the bridge through Rain in such manner that Walther's Division of the Dragoons had to take the rear of the column instead of the head, and probably as a consequence of an inadequate Cavalry screen Soult allowed himself to be drawn aside from the Augsburg road into a skirmish in the direction of Aichach. Finally his troops bivouacked at Mainbach, face to face with Austrian outposts, and a good ten miles short of his destination.

From these positions a concentration at Augsburg on the 9th was entirely out of the question.

Murat, with four Divisions of Cavalry very widely distrib-

2. The 4th Division, the last of Soult's Corps, was at Nordlingen on the 7th and only due to arrive at Donauwörth on the 8th.

uted, scouted west towards Wertingen where, as we already know, they found the Austrian advance guard about 2.30 p.m. Lannes hearing the sound of guns, diverted the head of his column from Thurheim, about 5 miles south of Münster, and at once marched to support Prince Murat. The result of the combat has been already told. It broke off too late for pursuit, and the French bivouacked for the night in and around Wertingen, outposts close on the heels of the Austrians about Zumarshausen and Hausen. The information collected during these engagements was duly sent to the Emperor, but its influence on his movements is not to be traced.

Summarised, the result of the day's marching was to bring Bernadotte to Eichstaedt, Marmont to Nassenfels, Davout to Neuburg, Guard and headquarters to Donauwörth, Soult to Mainbach. Walther was between Mainbach and Muhlhausen. Saint Hilaire (of Soult's Corps), Lannes and Murat were between Wertingen and Hausen, Ney's Corps and Bourcier between Gundelfingen and Heidenheim.

The following extract from the Memoirs of Baron Thiebault, gives an interesting sidelight on the actual execution of orders in the Grand Army:

> On the 8th October we resumed our march on Landsberg. We had 24 miles to cover and had marched 15 when De Segur (A.D.C. to the Emperor) overtook us and handed over a letter to General Saint-Hilaire who was riding with Morand and myself at the head of my brigade. To my astonishment he read it out aloud as follows:
>
> > *General Saint-Hilaire,*
> > I send you this letter to inform you that the enemy occupies Landsberg. I think you can give a good account of him, and I pray God to have you in his sacred keeping.
> > *Napoleon*

'Come, gentlemen,' said the General, 'let us push on and justify the confidence of the Emperor;' and the troops, informed of the contents of his Majesty's letter, stepped out singing and shouting *'Vive l'Empereur!'*

Hardly a quarter of an hour had elapsed when an A.D.C. from Murat, urging his horse as fast as its exhaustion and the state of the country allowed, appeared on our right, making signs and shouting to us to stop the troops. The order to halt was given, and he informed us that the Prince was engaged against superior numbers, and ordered us to rejoin him with all haste.

'Impossible!' replied Saint-Hilaire, 'here are the Emperor's orders.'

'The decision lies at Ulm,' said the A.D.C., 'and not at Landsberg; and besides, what will be your fate if the Prince is crushed, and Mack forces a passage?' and as these reasons were backed up by the sound of heavy firing from the direction of Mindelheim, he insisted we had not a moment to lose.

Saint-Hilaire appealed to us for advice, and as his eye caught mine I said, 'General, march to the sound of the guns,' and this old adage, which will re-echo in the ears of Marshal Grouchy for the rest of his life, decided him.

He at once gave the order 'Heads of columns right wheel.'

The A.D.C. hastened to rejoin Murat and we followed in five columns.

We had hardly gone another quarter of an hour when again the command: 'Halt!' rang out. Murat's A.D.C. had disappeared, the noise of the firing had dropped, and Saint-Hilaire having nothing before his eyes to hold his attention, changed his mind. He called us together, and explained that we were disobeying a written order of the Emperor's in favour of an order from someone without authority to issue orders to us; that we might cause a superb manoeuvre to miscarry, and thus lose an opportunity of distinguishing ourselves, etc., etc.

Finally he ordered us 'Heads of columns left wheel.'

And so after three quarters of an hour wasted and a toilsome couple of miles over ploughed up country we resumed our march for Landsberg, in anything but the best of humours.

Hardly had we struck the high road again, when the sound of heavy firing was renewed, and this time it sounded much closer; in fact we could distinguish musketry. We might already have reached the Prince, and our failure to reinforce him might have gravely compromised him. These reflections escaped neither us nor the men, who as infallible judges felt the wrong done in failing to keep a pledge thus given. A general murmur arose and poor Saint-Hilaire once more changed his mind.

The Division accordingly changed its direction for the third time within the hour, with the result that we reached the ground too late to be of service, and were very coldly received, found no one to help us out with food or shelter, and our men passed a bitterly cold night in bivouac. When at length the next evening we did arrive in Landsberg; soaked to the very bones, and utterly worn out, we discovered that by superior order all our baggage had been sent back to Augsburg. Thus I found myself without my second horse, without a servant, and without even a dry shirt, or a pair of boots to change into.

9th October. In spite of the testimony of the prisoners taken at Wertingen, to the effect that from 60,000 to 70,000 Austrians lay between them and the Iller, the Emperor persisted in his opinion that Mack meditated a retreat on Augsburg and Landsberg; thus he renewed his orders for the concentration about the former town of Soult (IV. Corps), Davout (III.

Corps), Lannes (V. Corps), and Marmont (II. Corps). Bernadotte (I. Corps) was directed on Munich, to take over the Bavarian Government and scatter any Austrian detachments in the vicinity, whilst Ney (VI. Corps) was directed to continue to observe Ulm, but to note that there were but 3000 to 4000 men in that place, and that he could give most essential help by co-operating with the rest of the army towards Augsburg. During the night of the 8th and 9th October, Berthier amplified this idea by the following letter:

> Soult is marching on Augsburg; it is therefore essential that you should arrive promptly at Günzburg, in order to intercept all movements of the enemy whether from Ulm to Augsburg, or from Ulm to Donauwörth. Be very careful, if the enemy manoeuvres on the right bank, to move rapidly and parallel to him. Throw Gazan's Division on the right bank. . . . In a word you are charged with the observation of the Corps at Ulm; if it marches towards Donauwörth, you are to follow it; if it marches on Augsburg equally you must follow it.

This letter can hardly be cited as an example of lucidity, and Ney being on the spot was more impressed with the possibilities of the Austrian forces around Ulm than was either the Emperor or Berthier. Hence, instead of obeying the order literally, he sent Dupont to Albeck, Loison to Langenau, Malher to Günzburg, and kept Gazan on the right bank of the river near Gundelfingen. The dismounted Dragoons were still scouting to the north-west about Herbrechtingen. The position of the remaining Division is not given, but it also was kept on the left bank.

In the afternoon Berthier wrote again to Ney in the same strain, insisting that both Gazan and the dismounted Dragoons (as to whose whereabouts he appears to have been entirely misinformed), should both march on Augsburg; he concluded:

> As far as Ulm is concerned, it is impossible that it can be occupied by more than 3000 to 4000 men, *send a Division to drive them out.* If they prove to be stronger, march yourself with all your army, capture the post, and make a nice lot of prisoners. Immediately afterwards direct your command, according to the movements of the enemy, either on Landsberg or on Memmingen.

At the moment that Ney received this remarkable letter, he had just fought a severe engagement at Günzburg, and had learnt that Ulm was strongly held and still served as a pivot of manoeuvre for the Austrian Army.

It was the central column of Malher's Division which had fought at Günzburg, and in reporting to headquarters Ney stated, "the enemy at Ulm is stronger than we had supposed. Ulm appears to form the left flank of his line of battle."

The V. Corps (Lannes) had been ordered to march first to Zumarshausen and thence to Augsburg—but fortunately it could not get farther than Zumarshausen: hence it lay nearer to Ulm than the Emperor's orders intended that it should do. Lannes was in touch with Ney's patrols throughout the day, and he also, whilst believing that Mack would eventually take the road to Augsburg, was convinced that for the moment he was in force about Ulm, and nursing the intention of attacking Ney.

The Emperor and Berthier, however, were not to be persuaded of the danger threatening them from Ulm, and the latter during the day particularly cautioned Murat to pay attention to the communication between Lannes and Soult, whilst Lannes himself was ordered to halt in such a position that if Augsburg was attacked at the break of day, the three Divisions of his command would be able to march to the battlefield at once.

On the right bank of the Lech Soult reached Augsburg by noon, followed by the Imperial Guard, and Davout reached

Aichach but Marmont was compelled to halt at Neuburg in order to feed his famished men. Bernadotte was still on the left of the Danube north of Ingoldstadt.

10th October. The Emperor passed the night of the 9th–10th October at Zumarshausen, but the time of his arrival cannot now be fixed. Here he was more in touch with Lannes, Ney and Murat, but their information had but little effect on his plans. Whilst admitting the existence of a considerable Austrian force on the Iller, he seems to have abandoned the idea of enveloping it, since Mack, in his, the Emperor's opinion, was sure to endeavour to escape to Tyrol, in which case the occupation of Ulm itself seemed a poor return for the efforts of some 150,000 Frenchmen. He therefore decided to divide the Grand Army into three groups, of which the left, consisting of Bernadotte and the Bavarians, was to move to Munich, as already ordered; the centre, formed by the 2nd, 3rd and 4th Corps with two Cavalry Divisions, was to remain on the Lech, whilst the right—*viz.* the 5th and 6th Corps with the remainder of the Cavalry were left to deal with the Austrians about Ulm as rapidly and decisively as circumstances permitted. He himself determined to go to Munich that he might be at hand to learn the latest movements of Kienmayer's 12,000 men, together with the Russians. As this move would take him too far away from the right wing to supervise its employment, he gave the command of it to Murat, ordering the latter to move on Mindelheim with the Cavalry and 5th Corps. Though Ney thus came under the direct orders of Murat, the Emperor gave him special instructions as to his operations against Ulm. These were drafted presumably by Berthier:

> To seize Ulm must be your first care, as it is important from every point of view. His Majesty leaves it to you to march in what order you may consider best. Invest Ulm during the course of tomorrow. The dismounted Dragoons remain at your disposal; place them at Günzburg,

on both banks of the river, ready to move according to circumstances. Immediately after you have taken Ulm, wait for no further orders to act; move on Memmingen, or on any other point which the enemy may hold. . . .

Comment: It is worth while to interrupt the flow of the narrative here, in order to call attention to the extraordinary similarity between the grouping of Napoleon's Army at this stage of the campaign, with that of the German Army during the passage of the Moselle on the 15th August 1870.

Map No. V., at end of book, is merely an outline of Ulm and the Danube turned north and south instead of east and west, with German names substituted for French ones. For Ulm read Metz; for Danube, Moselle; for Ney read Alvensleben; and for Lannes, X. Corps; the group of Corps under Napoleon becomes Prince Frederick Charles's Army; and Bernadotte's column the Army of the Crown Prince. Though the distances and numbers are different, the form is almost identical, and the point is this, that this identity of form, as well as the similarity in the misapprehensions under which both Napoleon and Moltke were operating, is the logical consequence of the means adopted by both for obtaining information—*viz.* the Cavalry Screen pushed well out to the front. In neither case could the Cavalry "hold" the enemy. They could, and did, indeed report where they were at a given hour, but from that information no certain inference as to where they would be forty-eight hours later could be drawn. Hence both commanders had to work on "hypothesis" only, and curiously both accepted the hypothesis of retreat, as being to their minds the most reasonable. Therefore Napoleon directed his troops on Landsberg and Mindelheim, and Moltke sent his to Verdun and the Meuse. In both cases the conclusion proved baseless, for both Mack and Bazaine were tied and hampered by internal difficulties in their commands which led them to a totally different line of conduct to that which their adversaries had thought out for them. So far at least in this campaign it is clear that Napoleon had not yet grasped the idea that he subsequently originated. *"On ne manoeuvre pas qu'autour d'un point fixe."*

Gazan's Division was handed over to Lannes, and directed to follow that Marshal to Mindelheim on the 11th October.

11th October. It was late in the evening before Ney issued his orders for the execution of the task assigned to him. The order to Dupont's Division (1st) only directed that General to blockade Ulm on the left bank of the river, but it was accompanied by an explanatory letter worded in the following terms:

> You will surround Ulm as best you can, and summon the commandant in His Majesty's name to surrender. It is very important that your right should reach the Blau, where it will be supported in due course. You will occupy the wooded heights in rear of Haslacherhof, and will concert with General Baraguey-d'Hilliers as to the best position for his dismounted dragoons, who are to support your Division, and form its reserve. . . .

A further instruction was also sent off during the morning by Marshal Ney, telling General Dupont to provide himself with scaling ladders, with which to scale the walls of Ulm, ending with the following misleading information as to the condition of the Austrians:

> The enemy is struck with terror to a degree almost unprecedented; he is retiring on Biberach in order to escape into Tyrol, his lines of retreat via Kempten and Füssen being both intercepted.

The Corps orders further directed the Division of dismounted Dragoons (Baraguey-d'Hilliers) to move at once from "Stotzingen by Langenau in rear of Albeck" where they were to support Dupont. This order should have reached Stotzingen at daybreak, and as it is only 7 miles from Günzburg, Ney had every right to expect that Baraguey-d'Hilliers would be within supporting distance of Dupont by noon but luck was against him.

The Staff Officer bearing this order was also entrusted with others to Dupont. His instructions were, however, definite to ride direct to Stotzingen, then to return via Albeck and Dupont 's headquarters afterwards. He started about 3 a.m., and, the track that runs across the "Donau Moos," a wide desolate morass, being difficult to keep, he mistook his way in the dark, wandered about all night and finding himself at daybreak close to Albeck, he thought it best to hand over Dupont 's order first, and then to ride on to Stotzingen. This place he ultimately reached about 11 a.m., when presumably the General was at breakfast or had other pressing business to attend to, for the order to march was not issued till the afternoon. Then the preliminary assembly of the scattered portions of the command took so much time that the troops did not actually get under way till past 3 p.m. Then moving by the shortest way, though not by the best its march was so much delayed that it did not reach Albeck till after dark.

Comment: This is a good illustration of the old proverb, "More haste, less speed." The roads across the morass were clear enough in broad daylight, and the steeples of both Stotzingen and Albeck are clearly visible from Günzburg hence there was no necessity to use up a staff officer by a midnight ride under peculiarly dangerous circumstances; a couple of orderlies, one for each set of orders and *one destination only*, would have amply sufficed, and one order at least would have reached its goal sooner than it actually arrived, by at least three hours, the other being received about the same time. The difficulty would not have been met by sending the same orders in duplicate, for in the dark both would have probably lost themselves, and there is a necessity always to economise in horseflesh. But the point really was to entrust each order to a separate horseman.

Whilst Baraguey-d'Hilliers was thus accomplishing his leisurely approach, Dupont had moved off with prompt obedience to his orders at 11 a.m., and before noon, signs of the enemy became apparent. He had about 5000 bayonets, 11 guns and 1000 sabres, the latter broken up into screening detachments, but he counted on early support, and though the Austrians clearly outnumbered him considerably, he did not hesitate to engage them.

But they were altogether too heavy for him, and only the deliberate obstructiveness of Prince Ferdinand, related in the previous chapter, saved the French from complete disaster, and Baraguey-d'Hilliers riding up in advance of his column with a small escort, found himself met by a confused horde of broken troops, camp followers and others. These he promptly rallied, and eventually the French occupied bivouacs for the night in much the same position as that of the day before, a result which was sufficient to give colour to a somewhat bombastic despatch from Dupont to Ney announcing a brilliant victory.

Meanwhile, the remaining divisions of the 6th Corps had crossed over to the right bank of the Danube, and except for the somewhat disorganised detachment under Dupont (they experienced a bad panic during the next twenty-four hours) and the dismounted Dragoons, the whole left bank of the river lay open to the Austrians for the next forty-eight hours.

Comment: Setting aside the appalling state of the roads, and the terrible rainstorm to which previous commentators make little or no reference, the Napoleonic strategy had completely broken down. For the Emperor with 200,000 men at his back was pursuing a phantom Army towards Tyrol—whilst the real enemy was in a position to cut clean across his communications, in order to reach shelter and reinforcements in the north, and this hours before Napoleon could have initiated an effective intercepting movement, containing even a germ of success.

It must be remembered that the French supplies were practically exhausted and they could only exist by moving through country hitherto untouched by requisitions. The Austrians, however, still had some supplies in their baggage wagons, and thirty-six hours would have carried them into fresh and untrodden country, whilst the wagons of the second lines of the enemy's trains would have fallen into their hands; and the captured horses at least would have served their captors to live upon, even if friendly inhabitants had not come to their aid.

Meanwhile the Emperor on reading the reports he received from Ney, began to modify his hypothesis of an Austrian retreat on Tyrol. Already during the night of the 10th-11th October he caused Berthier to write to Lannes:

> All the reports lead to the conclusion that the enemy intends to fight near Ulm.

And about the same time, Napoleon himself amplified this idea in a letter to Murat:

> I do not think matters are settled in your direction. The enemy, shut in as he is, will fight. He is receiving reinforcements both from Italy and the Tyrol. It is therefore necessary that your reserve and the Corps of Ney and Lannes, altogether between 50,000 and 60,000 men, should march as close together as possible, so that they can concentrate for action within six hours.
> If the enemy escapes you, he will be stopped at the Lech[3], march then upon the enemy wherever you find him, but with precaution, and keeping your troops in hand. Take no chances, for the first rule of all is to have a numerical superiority.

In order to render this concentration possible, Murat and Lannes now turned off from the road to Mindelheim and

3. By Soult and Marmont under the Emperor himself.

moved towards Ulm by Burgau, which brought them shoulder to shoulder with Ney, whose Divisions on the night of the 11th lay south of Günzburg and Leipheim.

All through the day, Napoleon's hesitation increased. Whilst still thinking it possible that the bulk of the Austrians had escaped via Füssen, the evidence pointed to their continued presence about Ulm in growing strength. Napoleon therefore kept Marmont, the Guard and Cavalry in and around Augsburg, where his headquarters were fixed. He allowed Bernadotte to continue his march on Munich, and Soult to occupy Landsberg, from whence he reported several skirmishes with Austrian troops which probably gave rise to the idea of "reinforcements from Italy and Tyrol" referred to in the above letter. From the direction of Munich, Bernadotte sent in word that the information he had received pointed to the presence of some 20,000 Austrians to his front, and to the *arrival of the Russians* within one or two days but at what point the Russians were to arrive, he does not state. The whole tone of the letter was so apprehensive, that Napoleon ordered Davout to move up within supporting distance, and further sent the Cuirassier Division under d'Hautpoul to report to him in Munich with all speed.

12th October. During the day Murat and Ney had met at Günzburg, where the firing at Albeck was distinctly audible. Possibly influenced by Dupont's too sanguine estimate of his own success, it was decided to order him to hold his ground while continuing to observe Ulm with his reinforced command. This order should have been despatched at once, but as usual nobody seems to have troubled about it, and as a fact it did not leave headquarters until the morning of the 12th. However, long before the order reached its destination a very serious panic had broken out, the result of the severe handling which the troops had undergone during the previous day, and Dupont's command retreated to the Brenz. Thither the bearer of the order had to follow it, and found it in such a condition that it was impossible to move it again until the 14th. In complete ignorance that this order had not been, and could not be, carried out with punctuality, Murat continued during the day to move the remainder of his troops into positions for an attack on the line of the Iller next morning, riding out himself to reconnoitre the enemy's presumed position. This determination, however (which in fact would have been a blow in the air, since on the 13th practically the whole Austrian Army was on the left bank of the Danube), was upset by instructions from the Emperor, who had at last convinced himself of the impossibility of leaving the Austrians still at large upon the Iller, or near Ulm, before turning his attention to the greater danger threatening from the side of Munich. He now wrote to say that he was initiating a concentric advance of his Army upon Ulm, and that it was necessary to wait for Soult to reach Memmingen, and wheel in to the right. His concluding words show how completely his opinion had swung round during the last thirty-six hours:

> This will be no skirmish, not even the attack of a column on the march; it will be upon an army which may be more numerous than you think, and on the success of which, great results depend. I shall be there in person.

Later on he caused Berthier to write to Davout:

> The Emperor does not think that the enemy has more than 80,000 to 90,000 men, but he will attack with 100,000.

At the moment the Austrians could probably not have paraded 50,000 men, and 100,000 would certainly have been an ample superiority of force upon the battlefield, but otherwise 8 or 9 to 10 seems hardly an adequate factor of safety when "great results" are at stake. Meanwhile as we now know the Austrians were free to move off towards the Saxon and Bohemian frontiers whenever they pleased. They would have done so but for the seething discontent and mutiny within their own headquarters.

Nevertheless, even at this late hour, the Emperor had not quite emancipated himself from his previous hypothesis, for on the same date and apparently subsequent to the above-mentioned letter, we find Berthier writing to Bernadotte:

> The presence of Prince Ferdinand at Munich[4] causes His Majesty to fear that the enemy who was upon the Iller has escaped to Tyrol.

This, however, seems to be the last trace of Napoleon's indecision and may conceivably have been due to some confusion in the mind of Berthier, for during the rest of the day he was busy sending out instructions to Murat to establish or repair bridges across the Danube between Elchingen and Leipheim, so as to be able to throw troops rapidly across in the case of an Austrian move towards the north-east. But assuming his own estimate of Austrian numbers to have been correct, Ney and Lannes would have been the only troops that could have got across in time even had the Austrians only started on the 14th. We know that in fact there was nothing at all to have hindered their march on the 12th except the opposition of Prince Ferdinand and his party.

Meanwhile Davout was nearing Munich in support of Bernadotte, and the following letter was sent to him by Berthier to inform him of the Emperor's plans and the part to be expected of him in certain eventualities:

> On the 14th, there will be a great battle on the Iller, near Ulm. Marshal Soult with his Corps is on the march towards Memmingen. General Marmont, with the two French Divisions of his command, is also marching to occupy the heights of Illertissin on the Iller; Marshal Lannes is at Weissenhorn, Marshal Ney

4. This is not a misprint for Ulm as I at first took it to be, but I cannot trace the origin of the astounding statement.

on both banks of the Danube near Ulm[5], and lastly the Imperial Guard is marching on Weissenhorn. On the 13th all the dispositions will be completed; on the 14th (the day of the battle) the enemy will be destroyed, for he is invested on all sides. The Emperor does not think that he has more than from 80,000 to 90,000 men, but he himself will attack with more than 100,000.

This affair settled, his Majesty will at once return to the Inn; then Marshal Bernadotte and you, M. le Marechal, will be two large Corps for action, and the others will be your auxiliaries. The Division which you have at Brück, one march from Augsburg, will remain there, so that in case the enemy should force his way out over the Corps of General Marmont, or over any of the others, you can move on Augsburg, support the Dutch Division which is there, and defend the passage of the Wertach, unite your army and attack the enemy.

If one of the wings of the Army on march to the Iller is beaten, you must still march on the Lech to defend the other side, and give the Emperor time to make his dispositions; but lastly I must tell you that the bulk of the army which will be on the Iller can only be beaten on the 14th, hence it will only be on the 15th and 16th that you can be of use on the Lech; hence if tomorrow Marshal Bernadotte has need of you to attack the enemy behind the Isar, you can join him with the bulk of your forces; employ them on the 13th and 14th and return on the 15th to be ready to execute the possible movements indicated above.

In view of what I have already written, comment on the above is needless.

13th October. During the night of the 12th-13th October Marshal Lannes wrote the following very important letter

5. Rather a sanguine interpretation of the facts, by the way.

to Murat, exposing fully the Emperor's false conception of the situation:

> The enemy's army is on the left bank of the Danube: at this moment there is only a reserve of from 4000 to 5000 men in Ulm. Everything therefore points to an attempt to retire into Franconia, and I have no doubt the movement will begin tonight.
>
> You will no doubt therefore judge it expedient to march at once to the support of Dupont's Division, and to carry a great part of your force over to the left bank of the Danube. Personally I believe the need to be most urgent. Your Highness will, I am convinced, consider it advisable to inform his Imperial Majesty of the true state of affairs.

Unfortunately Murat, less clear-sighted than Lannes, sent on only a summary of the letters, with the comment:

> Although the engagement of yesterday in which Dupont's Division was concerned has shown our weakness on the left bank and our plans on the right, I do not share the opinion of Marshal Lannes. At daybreak I am going to reconnoitre the enemy's position; meanwhile I shall impress upon Marshal Ney the need of informing Dupont of the project Marshal Lannes attributes to the Austrians, and order him to exercise the strictest surveillance. . . . Your Majesty will arrive and will order the movement yourself; I cannot decide so easily, knowing as I do about the movements of General Marmont and Marshal Soult on my left. Might it not upset your general plan? I confine myself, therefore, Sire, to press the occupation of the bridge at Elchingen, and to forward you the information I have received.

Murat then proceeds to insist on the smallness of the risk in the direction of Albeck and adds: " In any case Dupont's

Division is there and we can count upon him, as he has just proved." He little knew that Dupont was not there, but miles to the rear on the Brenz, reorganising his exhausted troops, who were without guns or ammunition.

Meanwhile the Emperor himself reached the ground. At Günzburg, where he expected to find both Murat and Ney, he was astonished at the uncertainty which existed as to the position of Dupont, and after sending a staff officer to obtain precise information, he went on to Pfaffenhofen, Murat's headquarters.

But not even here could he acquire a precise idea of the positions of the 6th Corps (Ney). It was known that the Divisions of Loison and Malher were, at least in part, in the villages of Leipheim, Falheim and Nersingen; also it was believed that they occupied Elchingen. Moreover, as Murat had ordered Dupont on the 11th to remain at Albeck, he supposed him still to be there. The Emperor therefore contented himself for the moment by ordering Lannes to push on Gazan's Division to Pfühl under the walls of Ulm; then with the remainder of his Corps to capture at any cost the bridge of Ober-Kirchberg, and gain a footing on the left bank of the Iller, thus establishing direct communication with Soult. Marmont, who had passed at Krumbach, was to move up to Weissenhorn.

Presently the news arrived that Dupont had retreated on the Brenz, that the 6th Corps had only sent a small reconnaissance towards Ober-Elchingen, which had been forced to return by greatly superior numbers of the enemy, and that only three companies remained in observation of the bridge of Elchingen—*i.e.* on the right bank.

Then the storm broke. The Emperor reproached Ney with having sent Dupont forward on the 11th without support, with having evacuated Albeck and Elchingen without orders, with having failed to establish communications between his Divisions, and with having left him in ignorance as to the movements and positions of his whole Corps. Finally he ordered him to occupy the passage of the river at Elchingen the next morning—*i.e.* 14th.

Later, Dupont reported that he was surrounded on all sides by detachments of the enemy.

At night the troops actually occupied the following positions: Dupont still on the Brenz; Malher and Bourcier at Falheim; Loison on the march to Nersingen; the dismounted Dragoons at Leipheim; Gazan, Suchet and Beaumont still on the Roth in the same positions they had reached on the previous evening. Oudinot was arriving at Ober-Kirchberg. The Guards and Nansouty's Cuirassiers at Günzburg, Marmont at Weissenhorn and Soult before Memmingen.

14th October. During the night of the 13th-14th the conviction at last began to wake in Napoleon's mind that the true decision lay on the left bank of the Danube. Accordingly, he ordered Lannes to support Ney at the earliest possible moment, whilst Marmont relieved Oudinot at Ober-Kirchberg. Berthier then wrote to Ney in the Emperor's name ordering him to capture the heights above Albeck—*i.e.* the Ober-Elchingen ridge—and promising full support if serious resistance was encountered.

Dupont next morning made a faint-hearted attempt to carry out Ney's orders that he should reoccupy Albeck, but seeing an Austrian column moving by his right on the Nerenstetten road, "he withdrew to the Brenz to cover the communications of the Army by Gundelfingen and Günzburg."

At 8 a.m. Ney leading, with Loison's Division as his advance guard, reached the Danube and found the farther side of the bridge held by 300 Austrians and 2 guns. These guns were promptly crushed by a French mass of 17 guns, and under cover of this fire, the men raced across the road-bearers, the roadway itself having been removed, and soon drove the Austrians away from the farther bank.

The bridge itself was rapidly made passable for all arms,

and the infantry flowed over it uninterruptedly, though the passage of the guns was long delayed. Then followed a typical French Revolutionary Army attack. They were met first by flanking parties covering the march of the main body along the Heidenheim road, but these were soon driven in by the excessive mobility of the French, who thus discovered the movement which flankers had been sent out to cover, and at once bore down upon the marching columns. These in turn formed into several big squares, and still endeavoured to continue their march towards the eastward. Cavalry, Infantry, and the guns as they tardily came to hand, combined against these masses, and though, in spite of their exhausted horses, the Austrian Cavalry made many brilliant charges, the whole force was gradually shouldered off the road, and compelled to retreat towards Ulm.

Loison's Division, having borne the whole weight of the fighting, which lasted for ten hours, was too worn out to pursue, and went into bivouac near Albeck, whilst Malher's relieved it in first line and threw out outposts towards the ravine of Thalfingen.

Chapter 8

From the Battle of Elchingen to the Capitulation of Ulm

From the date of the battle of Elchingen, the two opposing armies were so intimately in contact that it is no longer convenient for readers to follow them in two different chapters.

After the disastrous termination of the Austrian attempt on the 14th to force a passage to the north-east, the Archduke Ferdinand conceived the situation as entirely desperate. To quote the French account (p. 205, Vol. III., Pt. I.):

> There being no longer any opportunity for an example, or for devotion which could be of real utility, the first consideration was to deprive the French of the glory of capturing a Hapsburger. If before this he had shown greatness of soul and resignation, he now showed clairvoyance, wisdom and resolution in his action.
>
> Seeing that the complete investment of Ulm could be but a matter of hours he selected his companions, formed up the troops which he intended to take with him, and started on the road to Geislingen, not, however, without paying a visit to Mack's headquarters in order to announce his determination.

Curiously enough Mack altogether failed to see the necessity for this desertion of the ship in its extremity. He entirely refused to respond to the Archduke's suggestion that they should quit the army together, and he also denied him several of the officers whom the Archduke had selected as his companions in dishonour, stating that they were indispensable to him (Mack) in his further operations. This indeed they very obviously were, for even if the worst came to the worst, and the place was completely shut in, an able and vigorous Staff was needed to ensure an adequate defence of the town and the consequent retention of a large French force in observation of the fortress until the Russians and Austrians, now gathering on the Inn, could march to its relief.

Ultimately the Archduke with his escort, consisting curiously of seven squadrons of Mack's own Cuirassiers, rode off by the Geislingen road, which was still open, trusting to pick up the Corps of Werneck, which was still outside, to the north of Ulm.

But he never found Werneck, whose advance guard had by this time reached Aalen and Nordlingen, capturing a French battalion besides picking up some provision wagons, and stragglers on the way. Meanwhile Werneck's main body halted at Herbrechtingen to cover the passage of his convoy, and also to wait for news of his colleague Riesch. During the night he received the news of the engagement and learnt that the French were in possession of Albeck. Seeing that the latter appeared ignorant of his presence, Werneck decided to attack them, hoping that the surprise of his sudden appearance would favour a further offensive effort on the part of Mack. Accordingly on the morning of the 15th Werneck formed his troops in two columns, one of which, under his own command, consisting of 12 battalions and 10 squadrons, marched on Albeck by Hausen and Nerenstetten; the other under Hohenzollern of 11 battalions and 10 squadrons, took a roundabout itinerary *via* Harben, Hermaringen, Brenz and Langenau.

Werneck reached Nerenstetten at 3.30 p.m., but though he

heard the sound of firing from Ulm and his advance guard informed him that they had actually driven some French troops out of Albeck, he decided to await the Prince of Hohenzollern's arrival. But the latter failing to put in an appearance, having been delayed by the appalling state of the roads, when night fell, Werneck gave the order to return to Hausen, sending messages to Hohenzollern directing him to rejoin with his column, which messages the latter never received. Early next morning, 16th, Werneck again set out for Nerenstetten, still hoping for Hohenzollern's support. But his advance guard came upon the French under Murat who charged and routed it, capturing almost entirely a couple of battalions of the Regiment Kaunitz. At the same moment Werneck received an order from Mack dated the 14th, the spirit of which he had already obeyed; a few minutes later came two couriers from the Archduke bearing his personal appreciation of the situation, and ordering Werneck to return to Aalen where the Prince shortly expected to arrive.

Werneck accordingly set his column again in motion towards Herbrechtingen, and Hohenzollern who had missed his orders marched on alone into the midst of his French pursuers with disastrous results. Presently the French advance overtook Werneck also, when a *parlementaire* summoned him to surrender, but was sent back.

The French then attacked his column which had scarcely had time to take up a position on the heights of Herbrechtingen. Though this attack was successfully repulsed, the Austrians bivouacked in considerable disorder and were surprised by the French about 9 o'clock that night. There was a bad defile immediately behind the heights and some 2000 prisoners fell into French hands. The bulk of the column however managed to get away and filed through Niederkocher from 3 a.m. to 9 a.m. on the 17th. Nearing Aalen a fresh order from the Archduke overtook them, instructing Werneck to join him at Oettingen by Neresheim and Trochtelfingen. The exhausted troops, who had been marching and fighting without cessation for forty-eight hours, now bent off from the high road and waded by cross-country tracks to Neresheim, which they reached between the hours of 11 a.m. and 3 p.m. They were actually at the end of their tether, the men sinking worn out by the roadside. Their chance of repose, however, did not last long. Within a couple of hours the French Cavalry again appeared, and the tired men struggled to their feet to resume their march through Neresheim on Trochtelfingen. But by the hundred they fell into the pursuers' hands though the remnant still maintained their discipline, and beat off repeated attacks of the enemy.

Only some 2000 reached Trochtelfingen, which place they found under water. Here the famished and extenuated men again threw themselves on the muddy ground to snatch if possible a few moments' sleep.

Then Werneck learnt the fate of Hohenzollern's command, and seeing further resistance was hopeless, he at last consented to receive a flag of truce and terms of surrender were signed at 11 p.m.

Actually only 71 officers, 1553 men with 31 horses passed into captivity, for nearly all the mounted men and officers had slipped away in the darkness whilst preliminaries were being negotiated, and went to rejoin the Prince about Oettingen. He, hearing of this final disaster, now made up his mind to strive for the Bohemian frontier *via* Nuremberg, which he eventually reached in safety.

From Oettingen the Archduke addressed a letter to the Emperor of Austria, giving his views on the situation in Ulm, and also his reasons for leaving the Army. These latter, I imagine no Court of Honour nowadays would consider as a sufficient justification, even if one could find a Royal Prince in Europe capable of such dishonourable conduct in a similar situation.

To return to the movements of the French Army. Whilst Loison's Division was fighting at Elchingen and the rest of the VI. Corps were moving up in support, Lannes (V. Corps) with the reserve Cavalry had moved by the right bank of the Danube up to the bridge-head at Ulm, brushing aside the few Austrian detachments which Mack had sent out for purposes of observation, his losses for this day being only 8 killed and 50 wounded. Marmont also reached his destination practically unopposed and stood ready to attack the enemy should he attempt to escape by the Biberach road.

Soult continued his wide-flung and profitless march to cut the Biberach road, leaving Vandamme's Division behind to overawe the garrison of Memmingen. These, some 4500 strong, were so disgusted by the poltroonery of their Commandant that they were threatening to break the capitulation.

15th October. During the night of the 14th-15th Napoleon made his dispositions to attack the Austrians in their entrenched positions on the Michelsberg and Geisberg. Leaving only Cavalry to watch the bridge-head on the right bank of the Danube, Lannes was directed to bring his whole Corps across the river by the bridges of Elchingen and Thalfingen so as to be at hand to support Ney on whom the actual assault was to devolve. The 1st Division of Dragoons, Nansouty's Cuirassiers and the Imperial Guard were to be held in readiness as a reserve at the abbey of Elchingen. All were to be in position by 8 a.m. next morning (15th). But there proved to be no bridge at Thalfingen, and the circulation of orders must have been even slower than usual, for though Ney and part of Suchet's Division attacked about 3 p.m. and succeeded in occupying the Michelsberg and Geisberg, they failed to make any impression upon the *enceinte* walls of the town itself. The two Divisions of the V. Corps (Gazan and Oudinot) as well as the Infantry of the Guard did not arrive until darkness was setting in.

Ultimately they bivouacked about Elchingen and Gottingen, and the Emperor's headquarters were established in the convent of Elchingen.

Dupont's Division had also been ordered to cooperate from the direction of Albeck. It left the Brenz at 6 a.m., but met the Austrians in considerable force near Herbrechtingen and Giengen, and was attacked in flank near Nerenstetten. Dupont had only some 4000 men with him, and though he succeeded in beating off the enemy, it was only the intervention of the 1st Division of Dragoons, attracted by the sound of the firing, that extricated him from a very perilous situation.

During the night the troops occupied the following positions: Loison and Malher on the Michelsberg and Geisberg were in contact with the enemy, with 15 field guns in action against the walls of Ulm. Suchet and Bourcier, with the greater part of the Cavalry belonging to the V. and VI Corps, had advanced towards Soflingen and Erbach to the south-west of Ulm. Gazan and Oudinot were in rear near Gottingen, and Nansouty was at Thalfingen, while the Guard was at Elchingen and Dupont and Klein were at Albeck. The dismounted Dragoons were distributed (chiefly on the right bank) between Pfühl, Burlefingen, Thalfingen and Günzburg. Only slight modification in these positions took place during the following day. It was during the night that the bridge at Elchingen was washed away by a fresh flood.

Marmont's orders were based on contingencies which did not after all arise, hence he practically preserved his position of observation to the south and south-east of the town taken up on the previous day. Of Soult's Corps—Legrand's Division lay between Dellmensingen and Achstetten, joining hands with the Light Cavalry under Murat. Vandamme was at Laupheim and St Hilaire, six miles in rear of Vandamme.

16th October. During the night of the 15th-16th the Emperor became anxious as to the real meaning of the several reports which had been received from Dupont during the previous thirty-six hours, culminating in the news of his narrow escape on the previous afternoon.

The country seemed to be swarming with Austrians, and

he was seriously concerned for the safety of his treasure, parks, convoys, etc., on his main line of communications between Ellwangen and Nordlingen.

He therefore sent his A.D.C. General Mouton to Dupont to obtain confidential information, and called up Murat from his Cavalry lying to the west of Ulm, to receive his, Napoleon's, verbal instructions, and at the same time he sent orders for the Divisions Rivaud and Dumonceau to move with all haste on Donauwörth, and to concert measures with the commandants of that town and of Harburg and Nordlingen for the most active surveillance of the roads to the north. These orders brought about the collisions, already narrated, with Werneck's column.

As the tactical details are of no special interest, except as regards the extraordinary vigour with which the jaded French troops, in spite of the appalling weather, responded to the presence of Murat at their head, we can now return to Mack, whom we left on the night of the 14th at the moment of the Archduke's desertion.

In spite of this blow, and the bitter animosity it had disclosed amongst his Staff, Mack was still very far from owning himself beaten. He had still some 22,000 men under arms, and though he was short of provisions, he believed at the moment that Werneck was well away to the north-eastward with some further 20,000 men, and by now was on the lines of communication of the French Army, while Jellachich had got away with another 6000. Moreover he knew that every hour he could retain the Emperor before Ulm was of vital service to the Russian and Austrian forces now overdue on the Inn. Hence, when in the evening of the 15th Ney summoned Ulm to surrender, he refused to consider the question, and posted a notice in the town forbidding capitulation to be even mentioned either by citizens or soldiers.

Comment: It has been the custom to hold this production up to ridicule because the events failed to justify the predictions which it. contained, but how many of Napoleon's bulletins to his Army on the nights before his great battles are based on better foundations of fact? Ulm, though only an indifferently repaired, almost mediaeval fortress (no fault of Mack's by the way), was with its strong garrison absolutely storm-proof. In addition to this, in the existing conditions of weather, the opening of trenches and siege batteries meant a delay of weeks, even if the French had had siege guns at hand with which to arm them, which seemed sufficiently improbable. Werneck, with some Cavalry, at any rate was loose on the French lines of communication, and Mack, familiar with French methods of requisition knew that this army could neither stand still on the ground they occupied, nor retreat by the way they had come. If the Russians had kept their time on the Inn, their arrival as reinforcements could only be a matter of days.

Generally the whole execution of Napoleon's manoeuvre against Ulm, the incomprehensible way in which he had flooded the whole country to the south of the Danube with men, leaving the north side entirely open for days, served to strengthen Mack's convictions either that the rumours of a British landing, and a revolution in France were true, or that the Russians were nearer at hand than he anticipated, and were giving the French more trouble than he had dared to hope. In any case 22,000 men were well spent in gaining even a few weeks in which the Austrian main Army could return from Italy and join the Russians. Finally, Mack was constitutionally incapable of subscribing to the lax code of honour which had crept into the long service armies in the guise of humanitarianism, which code justified a commander in surrendering a fortress without having faced even one assault in the open breach, in order to prevent the "useless effusion of human blood"!

But all these arguments failed to convince the recalcitrant members of his Staff, and seven of them Richter, Gyulai Stopsicz, Riesch, Prince Maurice of Liechtenstein, Klenau, the Hereditary Prince of Hesse-Homburg, Loudon, Gottesheim submitted to him this extraordinary effusion:

> We, the undersigned, are of the contrary opinion. We believe that it will render a greater service to His Majesty to obtain terms allowing the troops to march out of Ulm with their arms, thus saving a considerable contingent, than to defend this place obstinately, which is far from being impregnable to assault, and in which we can make no real resistance, as we are in a position to prove by documentary evidence.

One can only wonder what weight a French court-martial under the presidency of Napoleon would have attached to any amount of such documentary evidence. Only a year and some months later even the Prussians tried and condemned to death men whose positions were far from being as favourable as those of General Mack's.

Finally, either with or without the consent of their commander, the three senior officers Riesch, Loudon and Gyulai decided to send Prince Liechtenstein to Ney's headquarters to demand permission for the garrison to leave Ulm as combatants and to withdraw behind the Lech. Key at once referred the matter to Berthier, from whom he received the reply that the Emperor desired that the garrison of Ulm should surrender as prisoners of war. Liechtenstein returned with this message into Ulm, and the three Generals now sent word to Ney that—

> The garrison of Ulm, seeing with regret that the Marshal has not accepted the equitable conditions which it had hoped to have obtained from his sense of justice is resolved to await the chances of war.

Again Liechtenstein rode back with this answer to Ney, and returned at 10 a.m. with the declaration from the latter that he would use his best influence with the Emperor to obtain the following terms *viz*. a truce until noon, by which hour Ulm is to be surrendered, all the garrison to be transported into France. The officers and generals to be allowed to keep their horses and baggage. In case of refusal, the assault would be delivered at once.

As no reply to this summons was received, about noon Ney opened fire with his field guns upon the town, and a certain amount of skirmishing ensued. Presently a French *parlementaire* appeared, with an invitation from Napoleon for Prince Liechtenstein to ride over and discuss the situation. To this Mack consented, charging the Prince with some insincere and flattering message for the Emperor, but there appears to be no record of the actual instructions given him. Evidently, however, from the French accounts of the ensuing meeting, the Prince was to make the most of the near approach of the Russians to drive a good bargain for the Austrians.

Napoleon refused to treat the idea of the arrival of a relieving Army at all seriously. He said that but for the insalubrious condition of the district and its probable consequences to the health of his troops, he would willingly grant even fifteen days' delay to the garrison, provided that it surrendered unconditionally at the expiration of that time. Ultimately the Prince obtained the following terms.

1. The garrison to be prisoners of war, unless the Russian Army had appeared on the Lech during the course of the day (16th), in which case they should be free to march out to whatever destination they might choose.

2. The officers to return to Austria on parole, or,

3. If Mack preferred, Napoleon would consent to leave three or four Divisions before Ulm for five or six days.

Mack at first declined these terms, and there ensued an interchange of letters between himself and Berthier. But meanwhile in all secrecy Napoleon made every preparation to assault the place. This was a sufficient indication of the very real necessity he was under of becoming free to devote himself to the Russian danger, which it will be remembered had already seemed threatening on the 12th of the month.

In the end, Mack succeeded in obtaining a delay of eight days on condition that one gate of the Fortress should be placed in the hands of French troops, the agreement being signed at noon on the 17th to terminate at midnight of the 25th.

Accordingly, at 10 a.m. on the 18th, a brigade of Ney's Corps took over the Stuttgart Gate and immediately French soldiers introduced themselves into the town and began to mix with the people. At the same time the Emperor ordered the municipality to cease issuing food to the Austrian troops, and Ney set at liberty the French prisoners made during the engagements of the previous weeks. Presently the wildest confusion reigned in the city. French officers hustled the Austrians out of their quarters, French soldiers stole their horses, and as it became evident to Mack that his men must starve long before the expiration of the eight days, he rode out to see the Emperor on the 19th. Finally he agreed that the garrison should lay down its arms on the following morning, the officers being allowed free passage on parole.

The total number of prisoners taken in Ulm amounted to 25,365 adding to these the numbers taken at Wertingen, Memmingen, Günzburg, Elchingen and Haslach, the grand total of Austrians captured reached 49,718 men; a heavy price indeed to be paid by the Austrian Empire, but this is inevitable in the case of every lost cause. The real question to be decided with regard to this armistice is whether in fact the time Mack had gained by his manoeuvres was worth the price he paid for it. But this would open a series of questions far beyond the limits of the present book.

Briefly, the essence of the whole matter is this. By no other means could Mack have gained so much time, and if his superiors in Austria failed to employ this respite to the best advantage the responsibility lies on their shoulders, not on his.

That Napoleon was thoroughly awake to the danger of

delay is sufficiently established by the fact that he despatched Soult, Baraguey-d'Hilliers and the Imperial Guard, less the Emperor's personal escort, for Augsburg on the morning of the 18th, the moment he knew that the Stuttgart Gate was safe in Ney's hands. Then he expedited the march of his remaining forces towards the Inn, the moment the necessity for their further delay before Ulm had ceased.

Except for Ney, the whole army was concentrated about Munich on the 24th October, and on the following morning the march to Vienna began.

Chapter 9
Conclusion

To summarise the teachings of this Campaign and underline some of its lessons. It will be clear, I think, from the narrative that the doctrine of "re-entering and salient frontiers," of which it is often adduced as an example, had no part in the formation of the plans of either General.

Primarily Napoleon never attached any significance to imaginary lines drawn to delimit the frontiers of any state, unless a physical obstacle, or the menace of serious opposition by armed force, rendered it expedient for him to do so.

He would not have objected to Bernadotte marching south from Hanover to Wurzburg had the march been convenient, indeed he would have welcomed it as tending to relieve the congestion of the Frankfort-Aschaffenburg Wurzburg road, and thus avoiding the strain on Bernadotte 's men and the consequent delays. But he attached no significance at all to the fact that Wurzburg was on the Main and that this river joined the Rhine at Frankfort, making a re-entrant angle relative to the territory his troops actually occupied, for the fact that at the time he did not and could not know that Mack intended to stay on the Iller rendered this relationship entirely unimportant.

The real truth was that neither Mack nor Napoleon was thinking of their communications in the recognised eighteenth-century interpretation of the word at all, for both proposed in principle to live on the country they occupied, and Mack had been busy amassing magazines all over the districts either belonging to Austria, or over which Austria claimed certain rights, in order to keep himself as free as possible of the hampering conditions which regard for the maintenance of a rigid line of communications necessarily imposed. He was in fact preparing to use the country round Ulm as a temporary base, precisely as Napoleon used Leipzig in 1813.

The Emperor on the contrary, having no organised supply service, was bound to sweep over the widest area of the most fertile districts which lay between him and his objective, Vienna, and he based his converging march upon the Danube between Gundelfingen and Neuburg on the assumption that the Austrians would prove as susceptible to this threat at their direct lines of communication with Vienna as they had always shown themselves to be in previous years. He had no idea, in fact, how far Mack had actually succeeded in modifying the accepted views as to living on the enemy's country and making "war support war" in the few months during which he had been at work reorganising the Austrian armies.

It was this preconceived opinion which led the Emperor to misinterpret so entirely the information furnished to him by his contact detachments when they drove Kienmayer's troops before them at Donauwörth. His orders for the concentration on Augsburg and his persistence in regarding that point as the key of the whole situation, notwithstanding the warnings he received from Ney, would be unintelligible on any other hypothesis.

Mack's conduct, on the other hand, on learning from the reconnaissance sent out to Wertingen on the 9th October of Napoleon's movement towards Augsburg, would be equally unintelligible had he not been prepared from the first to find his direct communications severed.

As he had written at an earlier date to the Emperor of Austria, he regarded his Army as the anvil and the Russian and Austrian main armies as the hammer between which the French were to be trapped. The term "anvil" certainly implies passivity, but similes must not be interpreted too literally, and one may safely assume from his subsequent action that he was quite ready to assume the role of hammer using the Russians as anvil if the circumstances favoured the change. Moreover, at the time he wrote, it is not at all certain that he had any idea how badly his many instructions for the filling of magazines had been carried out, and it is at any rate absolutely certain that he did not anticipate Spangen's contemptible surrender of Memmingen.

In any case, an Army of 50,000 Austrians between Memmingen and Ulm, distant from one another only 35 miles, fully 20 of which could be rendered unapproachable by artificial inundations of the boggy peat mosses through which the Iller runs, and drawing supplies from the magazines at either extremity and the district to the westward, must have proved a very formidable obstacle to the French Army, unprovided as it was with siege artillery.

That Mack resisted its attractions, to which Napoleon had expected him to succumb, shows how greatly the latter had underestimated the character of his opponent, and if he escaped the penalty for this mistake of judgment, this was through no fault of Mack. I have related above the incident of the young Archduke's misconduct at the battle of Haslach on the 9th October in itself sufficient to account for Mack's failure to force his way out on that occasion, but there were other conditions fighting against him which deserve to be taken into consideration.

It has been pointed out that the weather had been unusually inclement for the time of year, but as this inclemency was uniform over the whole theatre of operations, it is generally assumed by those who have noticed the circumstance at all that the results must have been equally unfavourable to both parties and might therefore be left out of the equation. Curiously, however, geological conditions intervened to make matters at this period of the campaign far worse for the Austrians than for the French, and as the fact only dawned on me when traversing the district in weather of much the same quality, it may very well have escaped the notice of other students.

The time was in August, it had been pouring all night and very heavy storms swept over the country during the day. During the morning I had been walking over the ground on the right bank of the Danube, but though much water lay in pools, and the country roads were sloppy, they were far from being bottomless, nor did it appear to me likely that they would become so even under such traffic as the marching of the Austrian and French troops as recorded would put upon them. Even in the actual alluvial plain, which extends a couple of miles or so on the left bank of the river, the going across country was not difficult. But suddenly, nearing the slopes of the hills which dip from the convent of Elchingen, south towards the river and east towards Albeck and Langenau, I encountered the most viscous and slippery mud it has ever been my misfortune to meet. I thought Chatham had taught me the worst that chalk wash could accomplish, but in less than a mile I found I had still much to learn, and after the next two I no longer needed anyone to tell me why the Austrians had failed to escape—one's feet acted as suckers and I found my rate of progress came down to exactly that of the Austrian Infantry *viz.* about one mile an hour.

Now, as explained in the chapter on the Austrian Army, though the Army as a whole was slow, owing to defective methods of circulating orders, etc., the troops themselves were by no means bad marchers. As the incidents of the 7th and 8th October after the engagement at Wertingen showed, they could march as fast and far along the tracks on the right bank of the Danube as the French, it was only on the left bank that they failed to keep reasonable time.

A reference to a geological chart gives the explanation. South of the Danube the whole country is formed by the moraines left behind by the great glaciers of the Alps as they retreated southward. The "floor" of the country therefore is chiefly sand and gravel, and though the valleys of the Iller and Lech are abundantly furnished with peat moors, these are only local, and as a whole the district will absorb any amount of rainfall.

But an offshoot of the Jura formation stretches right across Swabia called the Rauhe Alb or Alp, generally barren and inhospitable, consisting of cretaceous rock, and layers of deep-sea mud—finer grained and more clayey than the Eocene sands which have been deposited upon the lower slopes of our own chalk formations—which poach up under traffic into a viscid water-holding medium of the most aggravating description. This ridge sends out offshoots which come down close to Ulm on the left bank of the river and extend right across country to the East and North, and it was exactly across this country that every Austrian sally had to be made. At Haslach, Mack had got beyond its eastern limit, and but for the Archduke's withdrawal would have been on equal terms with the French, but on the 14th October, the day of Elchingen, the decisive fighting took place on the very line of demarcation between the two surfaces, and whereas the French coming up from Riedheim, Leipheim and the Elchingen bridge met with no special hindrance from the ground, the Austrian reserves were practically anchored in their positions and hence could not support their fighting line in time. In fine weather I have now no doubt at all that Dupont's Division about Albeck and Haslach would have been destroyed, and even the whole of Key's Corps had it been on the ground, for 50,000 Austrians strong in Cavalry were at least a match for Key's 30,000 even with the division of dismounted Dragoons thrown in. Similarly I think that but for the delay, due to the mud in the Austrian march of the 13th, the battle of Elchingen would not have been fought at all, or if fought, then under far more favourable conditions for the Austrians than those which actually arose.

In either case it is clear that Mack's main Army would have got clear away, and the net so cunningly devised by Napoleon for the 14th October would have closed in on an empty nest.

I have already commented on the Strategy—*i.e.* the "Art of the Leader" which after marching 200,000 men through a mean distance of some 300 miles only brought some 40,000 men within striking distance at the place and time of the decision—let us now see how the system subsequently devised by Napoleon and employed by him with such signal results at Eylau Friedland (and many other battles in which not one man, horse or gun was not available to join in the battle had the necessity arisen) would have worked out in this particular campaign.

To begin with, the Emperor would never have ordered the intended concentrations on Augsburg and Landsberg on hypothetical deductions drawn from insufficient evidence.

He would have realised that the direction of Kienmayer's retreat afforded no certain indication of Mack's probable conduct and therefore would have focussed his attention on the main body of his enemy. Leaving, presumably, Bernadotte together with the Bavarians to watch the Russians towards Munich and the Isar, he would, I imagine, have formed his lozenge, facing west somewhat in the following order.

Murat—with Lannes and Marmont as General Advance Guard moving on Wertingen. Soult echeloned at a day's march in rear on the left; along the Augsburg-Ulm road, Ney with the dismounted Dragoons and probably a Division detailed from Lannes' command, between Günzburg and Gundelfingen. The Guards in the centre and Davout in support to close the square.

Murat, gaining touch with Mack at Wertingen, and acting with the vigour Napoleon after Jena learnt how to impart to his commanders, would probably never have allowed the Austrians to get away from him, but would have held them to their ground for 48 hours until Soult from the left and Ney from the right had swung in and cut them off from Ulm, or at least would have driven them into it and invested the place firmly by the evening of the 10th October, bringing some 20,000 men to bear at the decisive time and place and gaining 12 clear days in which to move against the Russians. Or assuming that Mack had succeeded in evading Lannes and Murat, as in fact he did, and then ventured on his sally to Haslach on the 11th, he would have met Ney's whole command probably about Albeck, whilst Davout crossed the river by the bridges between Günzburg and Gundelfingen to come to his support and Lannes with Marmont attempted to join in by the bridges above Günzburg at Riedheim, Leipheim, Elchingen and Thalfingen (the latter was not carried away until the 13th October), Soult and Murat meanwhile completing the investment of Ulm.

This would have given not less than some 60,000 men available against Mack's 50,000 on the first day, with another 90,000 ready for action during the second day, an ample superiority for any opposition Mack was in a position to offer, even on the assumption that the ground had been good-going for his Cavalry.

Comparing these possible results with those actually obtained, the inference appears to me obvious that at the time the idea of the lozenge formation had not yet presented itself to the Emperor's mind, any more than it had occurred to Moltke on the 14th August 1870 when he ordered, on a similar hypothetical deduction of his enemy's movements, the vigorous pursuit of the French Army towards Verdun and the Meuse.

Napoleon was only saved from the consequences of his reasoning by the intervention of his fifth element, "the mud," but nothing of the kind existed to extricate Moltke, and but for the splendid resolution of Von Alvensleben in attacking, against all rules of prudence, the whole French Army on the morning of the 16th August, the results would probably have been as disastrous to his reputation as the false concentration on the Iller must have proved to Napoleon.

Now neither of these men were even ordinary human beings, but on the contrary were far in advance intellectually of their contemporaries. Hence if, when both used the same method and relied on the same hypothetical reasoning, the results only just fell short of the ridiculous, the presumption is to my mind overwhelming that it was the system, not the men, which was to blame, and the presumption settles into conviction when, as time goes on, we find the method devised to replace it giving better and better results, even when the material available for its execution had sunk to the lowest degree of efficiency.

Contrast Napoleon at Lützen with his conscript army, and hopelessly outclassed in cavalry. He is surprised by the whole army of the Allies in broad daylight—yet he only gives four brief orders, and before nightfall practically his whole army is on the ground. Even at Leipzig with a worn-out army hopelessly outnumbered, his method still gives him a two-to-one superiority at the point of his own choice.

That the tactical victory did not in this case follow the usual rule does not affect the general question, and we of all races ought to be the first to appreciate the fact. Plassey, indeed every Indian battlefield, shows that numerical superiority, to whatever cause it may be due, is not the last word in the Art of War. The point is this other things being equal—war becomes a duel between the will powers of the opposing leaders, and friction will ultimately wear down the resistance of even the strongest human being. Hence that Commander who by the exercise of a method which needs only to be set in motion in order to deliver with mathematical certainty the first condition of victory—*i.e.* a numerical superiority at the time and place of his own choice—will reach the field with a greater amount of will power still in hand than is held by his opponent, whom we will assume to pursue a system which forces on him the onus of decision upon insufficient evidence many times in the course of a single day, and the two opponents being considered otherwise equal, the tired man will always be the one to break down first.

LEONAUR

CPSIA information can be obtained
at www.ICGtesting.com
Printed in the USA
BVHW080229241221
624759BV00007B/472